PROVERBS
A Man's Daily Journey into the Wisdom of God

GLEN BRYANT

ISBN 978-1-64079-208-1 (Paperback)
ISBN 978-1-64079-209-8 (Digital)

Copyright © 2017 by Glen Bryant
All rights reserved. No part of this publication may be reproduced, distributed, or transmitted in any form or by any means, including photocopying, recording, or other electronic or mechanical methods without the prior written permission of the publisher. For permission requests, solicit the publisher via the address below.

Christian Faith Publishing, Inc.
296 Chestnut Street
Meadville, PA 16335
www.christianfaithpublishing.com

Printed in the United States of America

Acknowledgments

I dedicate this book to my loving wife,
Jan Bryant.
She has been my loving companion for forty-nine years.
She has loved and put up with me through
all we have been through together.
She is the love of my life, my God-given help-
mate, and my dearest friend.

Thank You

Thank you to Pastor Rick Fouts for all his help and encouragement in the editing and printing of this book.
Thank you to Amber Fouts for proofing the text.
I also thank my pastor John Lindell for constantly preaching the Word of God with a commitment to preach the complete Word clearly. I walk away from every sermon with a new understanding, a clear challenge, and a deeper love for Christ.
I need to thank my life group for feedback on
the book, prayers, love, and friendship.

I am not a seminary graduate, an ordained minister, or a theologian. My credentials are being a man standing in the need of God's presence and wisdom in my daily life. God has proven to me that He knows the best way to speak His wisdom to me and He knows you well enough to speak to you in a way you can understand. Take this journey with me and let the wisdom of God come alive in your daily life. What He offers you is exceedingly abundant above anything you could imagine.

Contents

Introduction 11
Before You Begin 13
My Story 15
Chapter 1 19
Day 1 21
Day 2 22
Day 3 23
Day 4 24
Day 5 25
Day 6 26
Day 7 27
Day 8 28
Day 9 29
Day 10 30
Day 11 31
Day 12 32
Day 13 33
Day 14 34
Day 15 35
Day 16 36
Day 17 37
Day 18 38
Day 19 39
Day 20 40
Day 21 41
Day 22 42
Day 23 43
Day 24 44

Day 25 45
Day 26 46
Day 27 47
Day 28 48
Day 29 49
Day 30 50
Day 31 51
Journal Worksheet 52
Chapter 2 53
Introduction to Chapter 2 55
Day 1 57
Day 2 58
Day 3 59
Day 4 60
Day 5 61
Day 6 63
Day 7 64
Day 8 65
Day 9 66
Day 10 68
Day 11 69
Day 12 71
Day 13 72
Day 14 74
Day 15 75
Day 16 77
Day 17 78
Day 18 79
Day 19 80
Day 20 81
Day 21 82
Day 22 84
Day 23 86
Day 24 87
Day 25 88
Day 26 91

Day 27	92
Day 28	93
Day 29	94
Day 30	96
Day 31	98
Chapter 3	99
Cool-of-the-Day Experience	101
Being Saved	103
Abba Father	105
Forgiveness	107
Vain Imaginations	109
No Condemnation	110
Beside Still Waters	112
Renewing Your Mind	113
Fear Not	114
All Things Work Together for Good	115
Knowing the Will of God	117

Purpose

The book aims for men to experience the following:

1. For men to daily experience God's presence
2. To taste the joy of spending time in the presence of God
3. To learn to see through spiritual eyes and be less driven by our earthly view
4. To experience the value of a daily journey into the wisdom of God

Introduction

During my "cool-of-the day" experience, I got the impression I needed to write an introduction, or a "Please don't misunderstand," for my book about Proverbs. The Bible is not to be just a list of principles to generically apply to every situation, a script to repeat as a mantra, or a kind of "A scripture a day to keep the devil away." You are not looking for a doctrine to apply to every situation to make your life simple and keep you from thinking. This can lead you to miss the point of the book.

This was the mistake of the Pharisees in biblical times. They focused on the literal application of the law and forsook the personal relationship with God. The Word says we should "worship in spirit and truth." The Amplified Bible says, "Worship in spirit and reality."

Seek the living Word of God that applies personally to situations in your life. Use it to learn more of the character and nature of God, your foundation to developing a real relationship with Him. That character and nature are embodied in the character and nature of Jesus.

Begin to understand that grace is amazing. It is not just a phrase or a song but rather what God has done for us to comfort and give us security at our deepest level of need. He has established a pattern to reflect upon in our relationship problems and to provide the faith we need to press on and grow closer to Him, to become more like Him through our relationship with Jesus. When we begin to understand that Jesus really is a friend who sticks closer than a brother, that relationship deepens, and we begin to understand what Christianity is all about.

We begin to see how sin has separated us from God, and the only way to overcome it is by our relationship with Jesus becoming a reality in our daily lives. In our own strength and wisdom, we are powerless. Our hope and strength are embedded in our journey through life traveling hand in hand with Him. What an amazing journey it is! It is beyond anything we can imagine or expect. Please continue your journey through Proverbs and then broaden it to all the other wonderful areas of the Bible.

Make it an enjoyable part of your cool-of-the day experience. Do not make it a religious ceremony or duty. Do not punish yourself if you miss a day or if the Lord leads you to another area of scripture. It is something to come back to as you need it, for as long as you need it.

It is personal between you and God. It is a stepping stone to a wonderful journey through the Bible that becomes a living part of your daily life. What I personally need today and every day is the wisdom of God.

Before You Begin

Let's begin with the basics:

For this to make any sense to you and to be of profit to you, you must know Jesus as your Lord and Savior.

Read Romans 3:23: "All have sinned." I have sinned

Romans 6:23: Sin = death (but) God's gift = Jesus = eternal life

Romans 5:8: While we were sinners. Christ died for me.

Romans 10:9: Confess, believe, be saved

Prayer: *Dear Lord, I confess my sins generally and specifically to You. I know You died on the cross as a sacrifice for my sins so I could be forgiven and have eternal life. I confess, believe, trust in, adhere to, and rely upon You, and have come into the knowledge that I am saved.*

You, Jesus, are the boss of my life. I will seek a personal and intimate relationship with You daily. You are the Son of God and will take me on this journey through Proverbs and the rest of my life.

My Story

Dear God, I have depended greatly on Proverbs my whole Christian life. It has been such a blessing and guide to me. It has given me wisdom in my daily life when I so desperately needed it. I have struggled for years to develop a book as a daily devotion to get others hooked on what Proverbs has to offer them.

When I was discharged from the army and started my teaching career, I sought You to find a way for You to daily help me face the challenges of the job. I felt such a responsibility to help children learn, and at the same time, I felt completely inadequate to do well at the tasks you had called me to do.

You opened my heart to Proverbs, and I pray this book will be an opportunity for others to find what I have found.

I was a child of poverty who became a professional educator as an adult. The child of poverty was still on the inside, and the man on the outside was playing a role. Shakespeare said, "All the world's a stage, and all the men and women merely players." I was playing my part, determined to become that person.

This book is about a method that took that child raised in poverty—with most of his elementary teachers having no expectations of him being capable of learning—and that transitioned him into an educator who became the superintendent of a school district. If you could find one of my old teachers and tell them I had become an educator, I am sure they would say, "There really is a God, after all."

My earliest memory as a child was when my father left my mother to raise five children by herself, providing no support. In my memory is a scene at the back porch with him standing with his suitcase in his hand and everyone crying. I can remember thinking,

"Why are they crying?" Then he said he would be back in a few months. I was two, and I didn't understand. It was not the first time he had left, and I would see him only twice a year: when he visited us in the middle of the night at Easter and at Christmas, and he would be gone to his other family before sunrise for the next thirteen years.

I was an elementary student in the 1950s, when I was one of only two kids in my class who did not have a father in their home. My friend's father died in an accident, and my father left. I grew up wondering why my father did not love me enough to stay, and as adults, my brothers and sisters shared they had grown up having the same thoughts. It is common for children who have been deserted by a parent to have these feelings. It has taken some major healing from God to remove those scars.

I knew we were the poor Bryant kids, and my teachers reinforced my fears that I was not capable of learning. When my dad returned and took the family to St. Louis, I was in eighth grade and didn't know him. The school tested me and placed me in an accelerated class. I was horrified and stayed up late every night going over and over my assignments, living in fear they would discover they had made a huge mistake putting me in this class and discover all the gaps in my learning.

My parents were very unhappy together and were never able to form a relationship. Like my brothers and sisters, I left home as soon as I could. In my adulthood, God has presented himself to me as "Abba Father," revealing his great love for me and the wonderful plan He has for my life. He has healed the scars and taught me to forgive and love my father. I learned to share God's message with him, to forgive him, and to demonstrate that God would forgive him if he would seek Him. God has taught me that forgiveness is the path to healing and has commanded me to forgive others as He has forgiven me.

When I started teaching elementary school, I prepared my lessons in detail and went over and over them before I walked into the classroom. I constantly lived with the fear that I would misspell a word in front of my students or not be able to explain topics clearly in a way they could understand. I just pretended it was all flowing naturally in front of my peers and students.

I taught in an "open" school, and we were always in the presence of each other as we went throughout our day. Five teachers shared one large room we called a teaching pod. I had a frightened child on the inside who was always afraid he would be discovered as not belonging.

Every day, as I read a chapter in Proverbs, I looked for a verse I would need that day to know and be what God wanted me to be. I needed the wisdom of God, and I knew it. I depended on this through my years of teaching, and God greatly came through for me.

I experienced a love for teaching and success as a professional. I became comfortable and confident in time, and God gave me many opportunities to gain advanced degrees and new opportunities as an educator. During my career, I was a teacher, guidance counselor, guidance director, curriculum director, reading specialist, principal, superintendent, and college instructor.

I have always understood that God took that child of poverty and created opportunities and knowledge in him to be able to do exceedingly and abundantly beyond what he was ever capable of doing on his own. The key was my journey through a love of Proverbs that opened me up to the entire Bible.

Our journey begins in Proverbs. If you will take this thirty-one-day journey in Proverbs, your life will be changed. It may be the beginning of your daily Bible study but can develop into a small part of your study of the Word of God. You have to begin somewhere, and I believe this is the best place. Proverbs will teach you the wisdom, nature, and character of God. You have no idea what remarkable things are in store for you on this thirty-one-day journey that could last you a lifetime.

I am not a Bible scholar. This is a very simple common sense approach.

I do admit to you that as an adult and a professional, I still have difficulty with spelling. I don't know how I would have succeeded without spell-check on my computer and "wife check" in my life.

Being raised in the bootheel of Missouri has given me many colorful colloquialisms that have created challenges for me.

To me, a short *e* and a short *i* are the same vowel. A pen is a pin, and it is pronounced the same. It doesn't matter if you write with it or stick someone with it. *Wash* is "warsh," *chest of drawers* is "chester-drawers," *held* is "helt," and I could go on and on until you all would be rolling on the floor in laughter. When I go home to visit, it all comes back into my language, and I find it very comfortable.

I have been prompted to do a book on Proverbs for years. I have started it at least seven different times with seven different approaches. I tried to do a topical study, and I got lost in the vast quantity of applicable topics and verses that overlapped. I also tried to do a daily devotion book that divided each chapter into twelve sections, taking a year to go through Proverbs in detail.

I had great difficulty dividing the chapters into logical sections, and struggled with not feeling I had great words of wisdom on all these topics. I am not a theologian. I am a man in need of God's personal wisdom in my life every day. I missed the point with every attempt.

Finally, after all these years, it seems now that God wants me to introduce the idea of daily going to Proverbs and making that a habit in your life. If you are a new Christian, you need to let God speak personally into your life from His wisdom, and you need to let Him reveal things that are meaningful to you.

If I could just take you through a month and get you excited about letting the wisdom of God come alive in your daily life, He would do the rest. Why? Because it would be what you personally needed, not just reading what I need. It could open you up to a love of the entire Bible and what it has to offer.

CHAPTER 1

First Month in Proverbs

Day 1

On the first day of each month, read Proverbs chapter 1 and ask God to highlight a verse that will help you that day. Plan to read the first chapter the first day of each month, and God will teach you something you need. Make this a part of your "cool of the day" experience with the Lord, where you walk and talk with Him each day.

Today I am drawn to Proverbs verse 7 of chapter 1 (ESV): "The fear of the Lord is the beginning of knowledge; fools despise wisdom and instruction."

The word *fear* in Hebrew (yirah) means respect and reverence. The term implies that when a person knows God and knows He is all powerful, this will come out in his attitude and daily life. Respect for the Lord is the place to begin accepting the knowledge that this book of wisdom has to offer us daily.

Which verse spoke to you today as you began your journey through Proverbs? As you go through today, look for ways to use a verse to help you or someone else today.

Notes

Day 2

Read Proverbs chapter 2.

Today, I picked verse 10 (ESV): "For wisdom will come into your heart, and knowledge will be pleasant to your soul."

I picked this verse because I have found over the years that reading and trying my best to apply Proverbs to my life has shaped my concept of God and given me a peace that has made me secure. It has helped mature my faith. It has also expanded my love for God and the understanding of how much He truly loves me.

He is concerned about my daily life, and I have come to treasure my daily time with Him. I call it my "cool of the day" experience, like He had with Adam and Eve before the Fall. Jesus has restored this cool-of-the-day experience and makes it available to all that know Him.

Which verse stood out to you today?

Notes

Day 3

Read Proverbs chapter 3.

Verses 5 and 6 (ESV) stand out to me today: "Trust in the Lord with all your heart, and do not lean on your own understanding. In all your ways acknowledge him, and he will make straight your paths."

These verses spoke to me today because they are very important to my journey through Proverbs. My prayer is that this guide will start you on a journey through this book that will open you up to the reality of the entire Bible.

Step 1 is for me to acknowledge that my own understanding is flawed and cannot be the correct guidance for my life. To be what God created me to be, I must trust Him in all His ways and make His ways my ways. His thoughts are higher than mine, and Proverbs will help me to understand God's message.

Which verse stands out to you today?

Notes

Day 4

Read Proverbs chapter 4.

Verse 18 (ESV) is important to me today: "But the path of the righteous is like the light of dawn, which shines brighter and brighter until full day."

When I was a small child, we lived in a very small town. I remember a time before we had streetlights. Our only light in each room came from a single light bulb that hung from the middle of the ceiling with a string attached to it, except for the living room that had one wall plug for a table lamp. All the wiring was exterior wiring. At night, when we went to bed and the lights were out over the town, we experienced a real absence of light. Today, however, with streetlights and other light sources on all the time, we do not often experience the complete absence of light in our lives.

In biblical times, people understood this verse clearly. It is very easy to get confused about the direction you are moving in the dark. The light of dawn and the full-day brightness are precious.

My journey through Proverbs has been like the light of dawn that leads me toward a brighter understanding from God's Son, like the full-day sun. I have come to treasure the wisdom of God in my life.

Which verse in this chapter is important to you?

Notes

Day 5

Read chapter 5 in Proverbs.

Today, I highlight verses 11 and 12 (ESV): "At the end of your life you groan when your flesh and body are consumed and you say, How I hated discipline, and my heart despised reproof."

The chapter is a strong warning against adultery and in general gives good instruction to make you have peace of mind, a healthy life, and no regrets. To know that God is aware of every detail of your life and every thought you have can be terrifying or comforting, depending upon where you are in your relationship with Him.

I could relate to the word *groaning* because the older I get, the more I have to groan about. It's like the old saying "If I had known I would live this long, I would have taken better care of my body."

I don't know where you are or what experiences you have had. Have you ever sat beside a friend's bed and held his hand as he looked at you and stepped into eternity? I have, and I am letting you know it can be a peaceful, grace-filled time if you and your friend have an intimate relationship with Christ. I promise that you will not be concerned about how much money you made, how important your job was, or how many degrees you earned.

Which verse do you highlight today?

Notes

Day 6

Read chapter 6 in Proverbs.

Today, I am going to share verse 19 (ESV): "A false witness who breathes out lies, and one who sows discord among brothers."

Discord is disagreement between people, and to sow is to scatter something. According to these verses, the Lord hates haughty eyes, a lying tongue, hands that shed innocent blood, a heart that devises wicked plans, feet that run to evil, a liar, and He really, really hates one who sows discord among the brethren.

As we get older, we can get very set in our ways. Our preferences about food, music, dress, worship style, different Bible translations, etc., can be very strong. We sometimes have trouble telling the difference between our preferences and our biblical-based theology.

When we disagree, we need to ask ourselves, "Is this my opinion [preference], or is it something biblical?" I have observed individuals speak horrible accusations against other people because they did not approve of their dress, music, style of preaching, phrasing, different biblical translations, etc.

Some have written detailed books blasting others, condemning them as deceived over violations in their personal preferences in music and style of worship. They are ready to send them to hell and sow all kinds of discord using very religious language.

We need to be very careful about taking the role of judge and sowing this discord. This verse is very plain about how much God hates it.

Remember, it was the religious people of the day who forced the Romans to place Jesus on the cross. Be distant from people who easily spew venom. Remember which animal is known for venom.

Which verse spoke to you today?

Notes

Day 7

Read chapter 7 in Proverbs today.

This is an entire chapter that warns against adultery. There are many warnings about adultery in Proverbs.

Why do you think there are so many warnings? As the kids would say, "Duh!" This is a no-brainer. Our desires are strong and can be a tool of the enemy to lead us down a path of destruction. Be smart! Be aware! Value God's advice! You can avoid destructive situations. "Be wise as a serpent and harmless as a dove" (Matthew 10:16).

Proverbs 7:2-3 (ESV) says, "Keep my commandments and live; Keep my teaching as the apple of your eye; bind them on your fingers; write them on the tablet of your heart."

These scriptures must become alive to you in your daily life. Know the truth, and do not get drawn into situations that will ruin your health, peace of mind, family relationships, intimate relationship with the Lord, and entire life.

Which verse spoke to you?

Notes

Day 8

Read Proverbs chapter 8.

Now that you have followed this pattern for seven days, I want to change the pattern. Each day, read the chapter for the day, select your verse, and make a note. After you have made your own selection, then read my selection and note. You need to make this transition to begin making this personal for you.

Today, my focus is drawn to verses 10 and 11 (ESV): "Take my instruction instead of silver, and knowledge rather than choice gold, for wisdom is better than jewels, and all that you may desire cannot compare with her."

The scripture reminds me of a scripture chorus we used to sing in church about God being better than silver or gold and how nothing can compare with Him. It reminds me that the wisdom of God is to be valued above any earthly gain or treasure. There is nothing that can compare to the wisdom of God in our lives.

When I was a college instructor, I used to tell future teachers that what I had to teach them would last them a lifetime if they embraced it and practiced it daily. What God has to teach us through His wisdom will last us an eternity. His wisdom is beyond important. It is eternal.

Which verse did you focus on today?

Notes

Day 9

Today, read chapter 9 in Proverbs.

I am thinking about verse 6 (ESV): "Wisdom says: Leave your simple ways, and live, and walk in the ways of insight."

This verse is perfect for me. The first thing I must do is recognize that my ways are simple ways. I have to do this often and remind myself of how much trouble I get myself into through my simple ways. When my wife asked me this morning, "Can you get some Splenda out of the cupboard in the garage?" I was tempted to say "Yes, I can. Can you get Splenda out of the garage?"

She was not really asking me if I "can." She was asking "Will you get me a package of Splenda out of the garage?" The smart thing, the loving thing to do, the thing to do if I know what is best is to say, "Yes, hon," and then get up from my chair and go get the Splenda out of the garage. It is to pretend to be the good man of God I am trying to be and keep my simple ways to myself.

God's Word can teach me His attitudes and His actions. When I start following His directions, my ways change and my attitudes change. It does take time because I am not always a fast learner and am sometimes willful and selfish. This example shows you that God is still working on me, and He has a big job.

Which verse are you thinking about today?

Notes

Day 10

Read Proverbs chapter 10.

I need to think more about verse 27 (ESV): "The fear of the Lord prolongs life, but the years of the wicked will be short."

This verse is true on so many levels. First, I must consider how the Bible describes this life as a vapor that passes away in an instant. Our earthly concept is that life is long and all we think about.

If you are a Christian and have an intimate relationship with God through Jesus, you begin to view life as eternal. You gain eternal life through Jesus's sacrifice, and no matter how many years you are on this earth, your life in eternity will be longer than you can imagine.

On another level, I can see how God preserved His people through the ages. Some Jewish dietary laws are not necessary now because of refrigeration, purified water, and modern food preservation. Think about how they preserved the people of God while others were eating food that carried germs and parasites. It shortened the lives of non-Jewish people. They watched the Jews live longer and prosper, and they were jealous.

On a third level, following His wisdom will lead to healthy choices that will not put your physical health and peace of mind at risk.

Which verse do you need to think more about today?

Notes

Day 11

Read Proverbs chapter 11.

I want to share verse 13 (ESV): "Whoever goes about slandering reveals secrets, but he who is trustworthy in spirit keeps a thing covered."

Historically, slander is the crime of making a false statement that damages someone's reputation. It has become so muddy in our world today. People seem to think they have the right to say whatever they want and that it is okay because the person they are talking about is a public figure. That is the reasoning of the world today, but it is not the wisdom of God.

When I listen to someone talk about another person, God's inner voice sets off a red-flag alarm, and He says to me, "Can you think of any earthly good that can come from someone sharing that information if it is true or not true?" He is telling me that I don't need to repeat it and that I also need to encourage the person speaking not to repeat it either.

Ask God to give you this alarm. It has saved me so much trouble in my life. I have often found out that the information was not true, or if it was true, the damage sharing it was huge. I have gotten into trouble when I did not heed this warning, and ended up hurting others.

Which verse spoke to you today?

Notes

Day 12

Read Proverbs chapter 12.

Today, I want to spend some time on verse 26 (ESV): "One who is righteous is a guide to his neighbor, but the way of the wicked leads them astray."

For thirty-five years, we lived seven miles out of town on a small farm. Neighbors were scattered far apart up and down the road. We were friendly but not close. As the years went by, we divided the farm into five-acre plots and sold them on contract-to-deed. As people moved in up and down the road, I often asked myself the same biblical question: "Who is my neighbor?"

Now we have downsized and moved to town in a small duplex. When I look out the window, I see lots of neighbors. God says to me, "Glen, all the people you meet are your neighbors, and now they are a lot closer to your house. What are you going to do about it?"

This has opened a whole new window of opportunity for us. We are getting to know our neighbors. We are baking cookies, welcoming them to the neighborhood, inviting them to church, learning their names, and praying for them. They may be thinking, "Here they come again," but we are having a good time.

Which verse did you spend time on today?

Notes

Day 13

Read Proverbs chapter 13.

Today, God is highlighting verse 18 (ESV) for me: "Poverty and disgrace come to him who ignores instruction, but whoever needs reproof is honored."

I have learned the value of instruction. I have also learned that there are two kinds of poverty: situational poverty and generational poverty. My poverty was situational. It is hard to break out of poverty, but it is extremely hard to break out of generational poverty because you are not given the skills necessary to break the bonds.

Poverty creates so many immediate needs and wants that you can become preoccupied with them to the point where you lose focus on long-term goals. To break out of poverty, you must be able to achieve long-term goals. Education is a long-term goal. You must discover that education is more of a matter of endurance. Endurance is more important than great intelligence. We all learn at different rates of speed.

My situational poverty provided me with a mother who drilled into her children some skills that helped break the cycle. She had a saying for every occasion, and many of those sayings helped create self-respect beyond our circumstances. We were poor, but we were going to be clean. We had holes in our jeans, but they would be patched. We would work hard all day; we would give a day's work for a day's wage. Our word was our bond and our worth, and so on.

With the Word of God and that foundation, you can see how I could begin to see education as my ticket out of poverty. Instruction is valuable, says the Lord.

Which verse did God highlight to you today?

Notes

Day 14

Read chapter 14 in Proverbs.

I am looking at verse 29 (ESV) today: "Whoever is slow to anger has great understanding, but he who has a hasty temper exalts folly."

This verse has been one of my most valuable lessons, straight from God's Word to my ear. Oh, how I needed this one! I learned that the Send button on my phone and the Enter button on my computer both needed a one-day delay programmed into them.

I learned that when someone made me angry, I reached for a blank piece of paper and a pen. I went old school, and wrote out my response. I folded the paper and put it in my top desk drawer and closed it.

I took it out the next day after taking some time to rest and sleep. Most of the time, I thought, "OH, DEAR GOD, I AM SO GLAD I DID NOT SEND THAT!" I could have created a big problem. If I still felt angry and needed to make a response, at least the response could make sense and sound professional.

So with the help of God, people thought I was a man of understanding, and did not really know how foolish some of my initial responses were. Thank you, God!

Which verse are you looking at today?

Notes

Day 15

Read Proverbs chapter 15.

Take a second look at verse 17 (ESV) with me: "Better is a dinner of herbs where love is than a fattened ox and hatred with it."

Herbs are usually dried and added to food to add flavor. In small amounts with food, they can be very good. Herbs served only as a meal would be very bitter and hard to swallow.

As awful as they would be as a dinner, they would be better than a tasty fatted ox where love is not present. An ox with hatred in the home would be worse.

It's something to think deeply about. To have a home full of love is better than any material benefits. What do you think?

Which verse do you need to take a second look at today?

Notes

Day 16

Read Proverbs chapter 16.

Verses 2 and 25 (ESV), respectively, are meaningful to me. They seem to be connected: "All the ways of a man are pure in his own eyes, but the Lord weighs the Spirit" and "There is a way that seems right to a man, but its end is the way to death."

Our conscience provides our moral compass. It speaks to us about what is right and wrong for us. Our moral compass is developed through our life experiences and cultural influences.

A man whose conscience has been shaped by this world feels that all his own ways are good. The truth is that the god of this world is anxious to shape our conscience, but the ways of this world lead to death. The Holy Spirit is God's watchtower, and He will never tell us anything that isn't God's will.

The Holy Spirit transforms your conscience into Christlikeness. You cannot depend on you own thoughts and ways.

Which verse is meaningful to you today?

Notes

Day 17

Read Proverbs chapter 17.

I need verse 28 (ESV) today: "Even a fool who keeps silent is considered wise; when he closes his lips, he is deemed intelligent."

My wife has often said to me, "People think you are very smart because you are quiet and have very little to say." I think she was saying that I am not nearly as smart as people think I am, and the sad truth is that she is completely right.

When I found this verse, I had to laugh out loud. Have you noticed that when people first meet, they often ask what you do for a living? I try not to ask that question but to rather listen and get to know the person first. They usually tell me without asking. Often, they say, "You are an educator, so you will know this or that." They might ask me how to spell something. I hate to disappoint them.

Sometimes they become distant because they have a preconceived idea about what you will be like, simply because of their past experiences. They may decide that they do not want to get to know you because they are not comfortable around you. This makes me sad.

Which verse did you need for today?

Notes

Day 18

Read chapter 18 in Proverbs.

I want to draw your attention to verse 21 (ESV): "Death and life are in the power of the tongue, and those who love it will eat its fruit."

When we were children, we were taught to say, "Sticks and stones may break my bones, but words will never hurt me." As we grow up, we learn that sticks and stones can break your bones but words can really hurt you.

I believe that the self-fulfilling prophecy is very powerful in creating a healthy self-concept or insecurity, depending upon the way a child is spoken to as he grows and develops. Many have spent years overcoming the feeling they were not capable of achieving anything. Be careful what comes out of your mouth.

God is good all the time. He does good! He speaks health and life into your body, and the better we know Him, the better our speech becomes.

Which verse did you need for today?

Notes

Day 19

Read chapter 19 in Proverbs.

I would like to take a second look at verse 21 (ESV): "Many are the plans in the mind of a man, but it is the purpose of the Lord that will stand."

I need to understand that the purpose of the Lord will stand and the many plans I have in my mind get in the way. My biggest desire is to clearly hear the voice of God. I want to filter out other voices and know without a doubt that God is speaking to me.

From my pastor's teaching and Bible study over the years, I am learning the following: (1) I need to anticipate God speaking to me; (2) I must determine to obey Him before He speaks; (3) He will never contradict His Word, the Bible; (4) when He speaks to me, He does not need me to work out any details of His plans; (5) I need to pray and listen for Him to provide specific details; (6) I cannot assume if he does something one way that He will always do it the same way; (7) My need to spend time with Him is greater than presenting a list of my needs to Him; (8) He will confirm His Word to me through wise Godly counsel and His Word; (9) the more I know about the character of God, the more I understand that His voice will not go against His character; and (10) an Internet search about the names of God and what they mean is a good beginning to understand His character. Each name reveals an aspect of His character. I don't have a complete list because I am still learning.

Oh, what a wonderful journey we are traveling together!

Which verse did you take a second look at today?

Notes

Day 20

On the twentieth day of each month, read chapter 20 in Proverbs.

Let's look at verse 3 (ESV): "It is an honor for a man to keep aloof from strife, but every fool will be quarreling."

This verse reminds me that it is not wise to quickly jump into a quarrel. I grew up hearing similar warnings like, "I am not going to put my dog in that fight," "There are always two sides to every story," and "Act in haste, and repent at leisure."

In Exodus, Moses stepped into a quarrel between a Jewish slave and an Egyptian soldier. He ended up killing him and burying him in the sand. He looked to the left and the right to see if anyone was looking, but he didn't look up for guidance.

Some people are quarrelsome, and if you spend time around them, you find yourself becoming more like them. You always have to make decisions about with whom you spend time. I always told new teachers to find the most respected, positive person among the staff. Make them your friend, and spend time with them. Make them your mentor, and stay out of the teachers' lounge.

Which verse do you need to spend time looking at?

Notes

Day 21

Read chapter 21 in Proverbs.

Verses 9 and 19 (ESV) give a similar message:

"It is better to live in a corner of the housetop than in a house shared with a quarrelsome wife" (verse 9).

"It is better to live in a desert land than with a quarrelsome and fretful woman" (verse 19).

When we look at these verses, we need to remember the New Testament makes it plain that there is no difference between Jew, Gentile, male, or female in the eyes of God. We could safely read these verses and substitute the word *wife* with *husband*. When you read the verse both ways, the message is plain, and now I am safe to proceed with the comments about these verses.

Deciding who you marry is one of the most important decisions of your life. You desperately need God's guidance. I have been so blessed by the wife God brought into my life. I have been blessed by her and the love of her sweet Christian parents. Her dad never introduced me as his son-in-law but as his son.

We always joked and said if we got into a big fight, I could go home to her mother and she would take me in. It was a joke, but I think it was true. After forty-nine years, we each share the same responsibility to be there for each other.

Which verse did you pick today?

Notes

Day 22

Read Proverbs chapter 22.

Look at verse 28 (ESV) with me: "Do not move the ancient landmark that your fathers have set."

Our forefathers have established one nation under God. Our constitution is clear that the rights we have are not government given but God-given rights. If you visit our monuments in our capital, you will see quotes on walls declaring that we are a nation of liberty, giving God credit as our Creator. On our money, you will find "In God We Trust." You can read Lincoln's daily journal and know how important God was in his daily life.

Educated people in our early American history kept journals. Through their letters and journals, we get great insight into their character and love of God.

Many teachers today are attempting to rewrite history according to their own agendas to delete the influence of God. They are willing to chisel from the walls of our capitol words that declare His glory and influence in the formation of our nation as a Christian nation.

This verse says to me that moving landmarks for your own purpose is wrong, whether they are stone markers on the land marking the boundaries, or words chiseled on the wall declaring how our nation was founded.

Which verse did you need today?

Notes

Day 23

Read chapter 23 of Proverbs today.

I need to spend more time with verses 13 and 14 (ESV): "Do not withhold discipline from a child. If you strike him with a rod, he will not die. If you strike him with a rod, you will save his soul from Sheol."

Believe it or not, when I started teaching, we could spank children at school. I started as a primary teacher, and when I taught third grade, I kept a Ping-Pong paddle in my desk. It was that way for my first eight years of teaching. When I taught middle graders, I had a little larger paddle. It wasn't much larger. It wasn't used the way you might imagine. I paddled no more than twice in a year. Several years I didn't need to use it at all. The ability to use it was more effective than having to use it.

The atmosphere of respect for the teacher and students respecting each other was much stronger than it is today. Many scriptures about raising children can be put in context with this scripture that let us clearly know that although we are not to be beating children, some children need a spanking given in love and not in excess. I know I was one of those children who benefitted from it.

Which verse did need to spend more time with?

Notes

Day 24

Read chapter 24 in Proverbs today.

I am thinking about verses 17 and 18 (ESV): "Do not rejoice when your enemy falls, and let not your heart be glad when he stumbles, least the Lord see it and be displeased and turn away his anger from him."

These verses remind me of the fact that when I was a sinner, Christ died for me (Romans 5:8). He loved me that much, and that is His attitude toward everyone. He desires that no one perish.

When we look at our enemy, we need to think, "There go I, except by the grace of God." Our hope and prayer is that one day they might understand and be saved. We are to take no joy in their troubles. The more time we spend with Christ, the more we understand His nature and character. If He is willing to give His life for us, He is willing to give it for our enemy.

We need to ask ourselves, "Is there anything I can say or do to help them understand how much God loves them and how He desires to save them?" If we hate them, curse them, and rejoice when they stumble, how will that increase their chances of becoming a Christian?

Which verse did you think about today?

Notes

Day 25

Today, read chapter 25 in Proverbs.

I am going to write about verses 11 and 12 (ESV): "A word fitly spoken is like apples of gold in a setting of silver. Like a gold ring or an ornament of gold is a wise reprove to a listening ear."

As I go through this day, I want to be an active listener. By this expression, I mean I want to listen closely to what people are saying to me and try to understand the real meaning behind their words. I am accountable for every word spoken. God hears every word from every person. He is a big God that created a big universe, and He can see and hear it all.

I pray to have the ability to fitly choose words that will be of help to others, that my words might be more than helpful, and that they might be valued and bring healing into the life of the listener. If they are a reproach, may they be received in the spirit of love in which they are intended.

Bind the hands of the enemy, and shut his whispers so they may not interfere in the transition from my lips to the ears of the hearer. Keep my thoughts and words pure so the listener will benefit from them.

May my thoughts be your thoughts, O Lord, and your ways my ways, because your ways are always higher than mine. May this be a practice in my daily life. Amen.

Which verse do you need to apply today?

Notes

Day 26

Read Proverbs chapter 26 today. We are getting close to the end of the month. Is this journey through Proverbs becoming a welcome habit?

Today I need to look close at verse 12 (ESV): "Do you see a man who is wise in his own eyes? There is more hope for a fool than for him."

My thoughts today are that I hope not to be the man described here. I must recognize my tendency to think I have developed some wisdom, especially when I hear myself pray and present solutions for problems to God, asking Him to complete my plans.

He is more interested in my presence than my plans. He cares about our time together and knows my needs. His plans are better than any I can come up with. I need to be a better listener and stop being foolish enough to think He needs my plans in solving my problems. I am better at creating problems than creating plans for my Creator.

When I taught, I used to tell students that you cannot effectively listen and speak at the same time. When you should be listening, speaking keeps you from receiving the message from the one speaking to you.

I need to remind myself that this often applies to me when I am praying and spending time with God. When I taught, I would often say to the children to whom I was teaching, "I am speaking, and you are _____." The children would say, "Listening."

I need to spend more time listening when I am in God's presence.

Which verse did you need to think about today and apply to your life?

Notes

Day 27

Read Proverbs chapter 27.

I am going to study verses 23 and 24 (ESV): "Know well the conditions of your flocks, and give attention to your herds, for riches do not last forever; and does a crown endure to all generations?"

My flocks and herds are the things in my life that God has entrusted to me. They may be things, situations, or people for me to care for. I cannot be careless about them and expect them to endure.

Moses's life was divided into forty-year segments: forty years growing up and ruling in Egypt, forty years in Midian raising a family, and forty years leading God's people though the wilderness to the Promised Land. Each phase was preparation and training for the next.

I always thought retirement was that time when you had an income, did not have to work, and could sit down in your recliner in front of the television. You could eat your snacks and rest as long as you wanted. As I retired, I watched my friends sit down and rest until they couldn't move easily, and they often died shortly after they retired.

Now I have come to think of my days before my retirement as preparation for retirement. I am aware of the herds and flocks that need to be tended to. God still has many things for me to do instead of sitting in my recliner. I will be healthy and busy using everything He has taught me and prepared me to be productive during this phase of my life.

Lord, let my death be an interruption in the schedule you have prepared for me. Take my hand and lead me home—the home you have prepared for me. Amen.

Which verse did you look at today?

Notes

Day 28

Read chapter 28 today. If this is February, you are at the last day of the month. Half of the months will have 31 days, and you will have a chapter for each day of the month.

I want to look at verse 19: "Whoever works his land will have plenty of bread, but he who follows worthless pursuits will have plenty of poverty."

I have needed God's wisdom to keep my hand to the plow and not be distracted with worthless pursuits. Several times, opportunities have presented themselves as a way of making lots of money.

You had to sell a product and get others to buy and sell the product. You found yourself working all the hours after your regular job to just break even while the one who talked you into this was making money off your sales, and the one who talked him into selling was making money off his and your selling. It went on and on up the line, and you were laboring, not gaining. You became so busy you had no time for your family, and your regular job suffered.

Does this sound familiar to anyone? Then you hear God say in a still, small voice, "You are not a slave unless you make yourself a slave to others. Stop this, attend to the plow I have provided for you, and prosper."

Which verse did you need for today?

Notes

Day 29

Read chapter 29 in Proverbs today. I am praying that this journey through Proverbs is becoming a blessing to you.

Verse 7 is important to me today (ESV): "A righteous man knows the rights of the poor; A wicked man does not understand such knowledge."

In our community, there is an organization named the Least of These. As I read through the Bible, I see references that show that when we minister to the poor, we are ministering to God. The wisdom of God does not make sense to the world, but God loves and values every person the same. He is not a respecter of persons. Every person needs respect. We have the same basic need to be loved. In each person is a God-shaped vacuum that only God can fill.

When someone comes to visit our church, they are not to be given a place of prominence just because of their wealth. We are to respect and treat people equally—poor or rich—if we understand the character and nature of God. Jesus gave His life as a sacrifice for everyone who will place their faith in Him. Rich or poor, they are all to be welcomed home.

Which verse is important to you today?

Notes

Day 30

Read chapter 30 in Proverbs today.

I will focus on verses 5 and 6 (ESV): "Every word of God proves true; he is a shield to those who take refuge in him. Do not add to his words, lest he rebuke you and you be found a liar."

God's word is always true. He is not capable of lying. I take refuge in His word and desire to know Him better by spending time in the Word. When I can apply His Word to my life, it becomes the Rhema Word of God. It is the living Word in my life. He does instruct that I am not to add or take away from it. His Word, like Him, is perfect.

The Holy Spirit is the great counselor and teacher, and is very willing and capable of helping me understand the Word and make it alive in my life. I trust God to help me every day.

Which verse did you spend time thinking about?

Notes

Day 31

Read chapter 31 in Proverbs today. This takes us to the end of our thirty-one-day journey. I pray it is only the beginning of your journey in Proverbs. I pray it will become a habit that will change your life and help you develop a deeper relationship with our Savior.

I am looking at verses 10 to 30. This godly woman has so many skills. Let's look closely at verses 20 and 21 (ESV): "She opens her hand to the poor and reaches out to the needy. She is not afraid of snow for her household, for all her household are clothed with scarlet."

There are many scriptures I love in this last chapter. The description of the woman who fears the Lord is wonderful. This woman is to be greatly admired. She is very capable to buy and sell and to make land contracts, and she cares for her family.

God took a rib from Adam's side so his mate could walk beside him as an equal partner in all they do together. She assumes great responsibility. A man is greatly favored by God to have a helpmate with many skills, willing to work together with him and accept great responsibilities.

Which verse did you study?

Notes

Proverbs
A Daily Journal into the Wisdom of God

Journal Worksheet

Month: _____
Day of the Month: _____
Year: _____
Verse Selected:

Notes

CHAPTER 2

Second Month in Proverbs

Introduction to Chapter 2

The purpose for this book was born out of my joy in my cool-of-the-day experiences with my Lord. It was also born out of the observation that women's ministries within most churches seem to be stronger than the men's ministry. I have always been puzzled by this. I feel God has led me to create a path to a deeper walk with God for men or women who would read this book and apply the concepts to their lives.

Many years ago, I participated in the Million Men March in Washington DC. To be standing by the Washington Monument singing and praying with a million men was an awesome experience. The presence of God was very strong, and we were making a statement about how much we love our God and our country. I had a deep appreciation for living in a county where we could openly gather and express our love and commitment to our Lord and Savior Jesus Christ.

It is so easy for a man to become so busy with the tasks at hand daily and not be in the kind of communication with God to affect his daily life. To not be aware of how much he loves us and wants to be close to us. To be close takes some time commitment, effort, and a level of commitment that I have not always had.

Now that I am retired, I have more time to think about the things of God and have become so dependent upon my time with him. I have come to look forward to it. He has brought a new awareness of how much he desires to spend time with me.

I say I have more time, but the reality is I have twenty-four hours in a day, just like I always had. I just have come into a new awareness and a deeper relationship because I have learned to prioritize my time and experience the benefits of my daily walks with our Lord.

I have been led to include a chapter 2 and 3 to complete this appeal to all who know Jesus to spend time daily with him and seek his constant presence in our lives. Chapter 2 will be another month in Proverbs. I pray after spending two months in daily communion with God it will become an experience that will draw you back to the cool-of-the-day experience.

The cool-of-the-day is not a specific time of the day. It is your time of the day you spend with the Lord. The Lord came to spend time daily with Adam and Eve because he loved them, and he has the same love for you and me.

The final chapter will be some notes from special cool-of-the-day experiences I have had. Some may be from Proverbs and others from scriptures God has lead me to explore; I sometimes follow cross-references from Proverbs, ideas from friends, and sermons that have been personally meaningful to me. They come out of my daily Bible reading and prayer time with God.

I pray that the development of an experience with God daily will be a life-changing experience for you.

Day 1

Read chapter 1 in Proverbs.

Today, I am looking at verse 23 (ESV): "If you turn at my reproof, behold I will pour out my spirit to you; I will make my words known to you."

Most of us have chosen to forget our junior high years when we were thirteen and fourteen years old. Our hormones were raging. I taught in a junior high school for years and am very aware of the trials and tribulations of that age and the ability to pass through this and move on to an age of reason. Some men have gotten stuck in that stage of their life and carried that immature thinking into adulthood.

This verse speaks strongly to that issue. We do not want to hear reproof and correction, but we desperately need most what we may not want. We need to be still and know God. There are high benefits to reproof. He will "pour out His spirit" on us. The Word will be made known to us. His wisdom will begin to make sense to us. A wall that blocks wisdom will crumble, and His wisdom will bring great peace to our life.

In 1 Corinthians 13:11, it says, "When I was a child, I spoke like a child, I thought like a child, I reasoned like a child. When I became a man, I gave up childish ways." Today, Lord, help me to know what it truly means to be a man and to give up childish ways.

Which verse did you look at today?

Notes

Day 2

Read chapter 2 in Proverbs.

Today, I highlight verse 6 (ESV, emphasis mine): "For the Lord gives wisdom; from his mouth comes *knowledge* and *understanding*."

When I think of knowledge, I think of facts and important information. The Lord provides this from his Word, and I can take this in daily. When I read the second part of this verse, it brings out the concept of understanding. To me, this is the ability to take this knowledge (facts) and put it together in a meaningful way. To use it and meditate upon it, and apply it in my daily life. This ability comes from God's mouth to my ear. If I don't go to the Word and feed upon it, this cannot happen.

I also think about the powerful part the Holy Spirit plays in the process. He counsels me and guides me into an understanding of God and his Word. This is what I need today and every day.

Lord, please bring to remembrance scriptures I have studied during the day, as I need them to deal with every situation I face. I know I need to take them from knowledge to understanding and then application in my life today.

Which verse did you highlight today?

Notes

Day 3

Read Proverbs chapter 3.

Today, I picked verses 25 and 26 (ESV): "Do not be afraid of sudden terror or of the ruin of the wicked, when it comes, for the Lord will be your confidence and will keep your foot from being caught."

Several verses in this chapter give comfort and assurance that if you place your faith in the Lord your sleep will be sweet when you lie down, you will not be afraid, you will walk in security, and you will not stumble. As I look at these passages today, I see they are cool water to a thirsty mouth.

At this date, we are a few days away from a major election in our country. The campaign is the worst I have seen in my lifetime, and I am now a senior citizen. As you read this, remind yourself how you felt on this date or a similar date in your life. Where do you get your strength, peace of mind, and hope?

My security is in the Lord. I know how much He loves me. He wants me to have confidence, to sleep like a baby, to put one foot in front of the other, and to move forward to trust in Him no matter what goes on around me.

I turned the television off and opened my Bible to find this passage. This is what I need to think about today. I also remind myself that "Fear not" is one of the most frequent messages in scripture.

Which verse did you pick today?

Notes

Day 4

Read Proverbs chapter 4.

Verses 7 and 8 (ESV) are important to me today: "The beginning of wisdom is this: Get wisdom, and whatever you get, get insight. Prize her highly, and she will exalt you; she will honor you if you embrace her."

When I consistently put God's Word into my mind, it will lead to insight. Insight is an intuitive understanding. It is a development of a capacity to deeply see through the point of view that God has. I can move from my ways and the world's point of view to the view of the Creator, Father God—counseling spirit and loving savior. His ways are higher than my ways, and looking at my life through spiritual eyes blesses me and honors me.

Our minds are like very complex computers. I have heard the expression "Junk in, junk out." If you put in good, then good will come out. Romans 12:1-2 (ESV) says, "I appeal to you therefore, brothers, by the mercies of God, to present your bodies as a living sacrifice, holy and acceptable to God, which is your spiritual worship, Do not be confirmed to this world, but be transformed by the renewal of your mind, that by testing you may discern what is the will of God, what is good and acceptable and perfect."

Putting the Word of God daily into your mind and applying it as you go through the day will create insight that will renew (transform) your mind. Today, I need to think about God renewing my mind and giving me a better point of view.

Which verse in this chapter is important to you?

Notes

Day 5

Read chapter 5 in Proverbs.

Today, I highlight verses 18 and 19: "Let your fountain be blessed, and rejoice in the wife of your youth, a lovely deer, a graceful doe. Let her breasts fill you at all times with delight; be intoxicated always in her love."

When I young, it was hard for me to imagine my parents thinking about sex, and it was difficult for me to talk to them about such things. I often approach God in the same way. I had a hard time talking to God and realizing he would understand this part of my life. Like most men, I just departmentalized that part of my life and kept it to myself.

The truth is I didn't arrive here by UPS, and my parents *did* know about sex. God created us and knows about every detail of our life. It is not a shock to Him that I have these needs. Have you ever read the Song of Solomon in your Bible? It is clear God wants me to have a healthy relationship with my wife. He created us to enjoy each other and meet our need.

This verse in Proverbs encourages us to enjoy each other unashamedly and not take our need to another. I have lived long enough to see the wisdom of God. I have observed how straying has destroyed marriages and families. Instead of making a man's life better, it doubles his troubles. It takes him to the point where he has two sets of situations and circumstances, and he crosses a bridge of no return.

God's plan is always best for me. His advice leads to peace of mind and a secure home for children and a secure home for me in my old age. It leads to peace this world can never offer. Trust God to help you in the relationship with your wife to learn to enjoy each other and meet the needs of each other. Guard against departmentalizing parts of your life that you don't share with God. He knows all before I ask, so it is silly to think I am keeping anything from him, and it shows there are still areas of my life I am not trusting God with.

God, help me to trust you with all the areas of my life.

Which verse did you highlight today?

Notes

Day 6

Read chapter 6 in Proverbs.

Today, I am going to share verses 1-3 (ESV): "My son if you have put up security for your neighbor, have given your pledge for a stranger, if you are snared in the words of your mouth, caught in the words of your mouth, then do this, my son, and save yourself, for you have come into the hand of your neighbor; go, hasten and plead urgently with your neighbor."

Did you know that the Bible gives you great advice about finances? Throughout Proverbs, are many nuggets of wisdom about wisely using money and financial matters. These verses warn against cosigning a loan for anyone. If you put your name to the dotted line, you had better be able to pay. If they need you to sign, that means their credit is not good, and that is a message.

I have cosigned for a personal loan and for a car loan. So twice in my life I have ignored the warning of God. Both times I have paid. It was either pay and honor my word or my credit rating would have been ruined. I bought a car I never owned or drove. I paid off a personal loan used to purchase things I never saw.

God does know what He is talking about. Follow his advice, and do not cosign, and do everything you can to avoid credit. If you can't pay off your credit card every month, don't use it. Every dollar you pay in interest decreases your purchasing power and decreases your ability to bless and help other people.

What is God saying to you today through his Word?

Notes

Day 7

Read chapter 7 in Proverbs.

I am thinking about verses 21-23 (ESV): "With much seductive speech, she persuades him; with her smooth talk, she compels him. All at once he follows her, as an ox goes to the slaughter, or as a stag is caught fast till an arrow pierces it's liver; as a bird rushes into a snare; he does not know that it will cost him his life."

Do you remember the saying "Oh, what a tangled web we weave when we practice to deceive?" When you go down the path away from God's best, it will often seem attractive, pleasurable, and great fun. On the surface, it may meet many needs, but as the story plays out, it leads to destruction and the loss of everything dear to you, and even loss of your life.

You must be able to play it forward in your mind and choose the path that does not lead to destruction. The way of the world is very seductive and pleasurable at first, but God knows how easy it is to fall into a trap. His wisdom will protect you and keep you safe. He loves you and wants the best for you.

What does the His Word say to you today to protect you and make your life better?

Notes

Day 8

Read chapter 8 in Proverbs.

Today, my focus is drawn to verses 15-16 (ESV): "By me kings reign, and rulers decree what is just; by me princes rule, and nobles, all who govern justly."

In America, we vote and feel we have a great deal of control in our government and in the selection of leaders. In other countries, the leaders think they are in complete control. The Bible reminds me of one basic truth: God is in charge! He is the creator, provider, and savior. He puts kings on their thrones and takes them off as he pleases. He does the same with our elected officials.

As we go through our day and face many different situations, it is important for us to remember who is really in charge. As we go and vote, we pray about whom to vote for and acknowledge that God is in charge.

On Election Day, as I was praying and I tried my best to listen for God's voice, I got the following: "The enemy thinks he is in charge, but he is not. Spiritual warfare is strong as the day of the Lord approaches. The enemy becomes more frantic, and some things must happen to hasten the Lord's return. Do not worry or stress!"

I do not pretend to completely understand all this, but I will as time goes by and the Holy Spirit continues to teach me.

What is God saying to you today that relates to your thinking and daily life?

Notes

Day 9

Today, read chapter 9.

I am thinking about verses 17-18 (ESV): "Stolen water is sweet, and bread eaten in secret is pleasant. But he does not know that the dead are there that her guests are in the depths of Sheol."

I once went to talk to a friend about leaving his wife and children for a younger woman. He was a member in my Sunday school class and I was his teacher. My heart was broken for his family. We met at a restaurant, and I was surprised he agreed to talk with me.

As we talked, the waitress hovered over our table too often, and they exchanged glances. I could tell she was too interested in our conversation. His story was strange but probably not different from other men who have been in church but confused by the enemy.

Don't kid yourself. The enemy can make the path to destruction seem so pleasant that you are willing to forget all what you know to be true. My friend told me about being really in love, like he had never been in love. She was young and in desperate need of help. It just started as a friendship where he was trying to help her. They fell in love, and he had prayed. God wanted them to be together. He knew it was right and it was God's will.

I was speechless, and silently prayed for wisdom. I could not believe what I was hearing. He had a wife of over twenty years who dearly loved him and two children at home who were teenagers and didn't understand how this could happen. They were all faithful to their church and thought they were secure. How could this happen?

The answer is one step at a time and ignoring warning signs until you are deep in over your head. Don't kid yourself: bread eaten in secret is pleasant, but it does not know the dead is there.

I looked him in the face and told him how much God loved him and wanted him to seek his wisdom. I asked him to give me one scripture that tells him the path he has taken is okay and would lead to a good outcome. I asked him to line up what he just said with the Word of God.

I told him the waitress who was waiting on us was his new girlfriend who was in fear I might say something that would discourage him from being her knight in not-so-shining armor. I told him if he continued on this path that he felt was so right and turned his back on his family he would come to great sorrow. It would build a wall between him and his children that would be almost impossible to break.

God loved his wife as much as He loved him. If he chose to desert her, God would not desert her. He would put the pieces of her broken life together and send someone to her who would love her and help God take care of her. If he traveled down this road with his waitress friend, he could never travel back. One day he would call and hear and feel the distance in his children's home that he would not be able to deny or get past. Another man would be answering the phone, one who was a good man whom God put in place because he loves his children and puts broken people together to love each other.

As time passed, he went his way with the waitress, and his wife became his ex-wife, who years later met a very kind man in church whose wife had left him. They married and were so happy God had brought them together.

I have always wondered if my friend remembered our conversation when he made that call years later and another man answered the phone.

When I left the table, and looked back, the waitress sat down to talk with him to make sure he was going through with their plan. She wanted him to raise her children, and he traveled down that path. She did not want this interfering Sunday school teacher or God himself to interfere with her plans.

What verse is God speaking to you through today?

Notes

Day 10

Read chapter 10 in Proverbs.

I need to think more about verse 19 (ESV): "When words are many, transgression is not lacking, but whoever restrains his lips is prudent."

Sometimes I write down quotes from people on 3×5 cards to help me remember some ideas I want to think deeply about. I have one from Craig Groeshel, senior pastor of Life Church: "Everything I say must be the truth, everything that is the truth does not need to be said." This verse calls for us to have restraint and be prudent about what we say.

There are many such warnings in Proverbs, and today, as I get drawn into conversations, I must be careful. Just because I know something is true does not make it right for me to share it. The Word talks about a man having righteous speech that feeds many and does not harm. It should be blessing others. The book of James has many verses that back up this importance of our speech and the danger of not controlling the tongue.

As I go through this day, let me be mindful of all God is teaching me today.

What verse are you thinking about today?

Notes

Day 11

Read Proverbs chapter 11.

Today, I want to share verse 4 (ESV): "Riches do not profit in the day of wrath, but righteousness delivers from death."

Sometimes, I clearly think I know what is best for me. When I get honest about a situation, I want to pick a path that is easier or I *think* is easier. I have often said such things as "Arriving a day late and a dollar short is the story of my life. I will be okay when my ship comes in. I seem to have too much month at the end of my money, and I have a habit of counting my chickens before they hatch."

There are a lot of old expressions that reveal my thinking has taken me in the wrong direction. If I have some money coming, I plan to spend it in several different ways before it arrives, and it seldom stretches as far as I think.

I often tell the true story about praying for God to provide the money for a bill that needed to be paid. In my quiet time with God, I feel like I could hear him say, "I already gave you the money for the bill, and you spent it."

Everyone laughs when I say this, but it really isn't funny. I think they laugh because they know they have had the same experience. I have finally learned to listen and manage money better in my old age.

Riches are what I think I need, but they are not going to help me as we get closer to the Lord's return. Righteousness is the path that will deliver me. It may seem like "The Road Not Taken," a poem by Robert Frost I have always loved:

> *Two roads diverged in a yellow wood,*
> *And sorry I could not travel both*
> *And be one traveler, long I stood*
> *And looked down one as far as I could*
> *To Where it bent in the undergrowth;*

Then took the other, as just as fair,
And having perhaps the better claim
Because it was grassy and wanted wear,
Through as for that the passing there
Had worn them really about the same,

And both that morning equally lay
In leaves no step had trodden black.
Oh, I kept the first for another day!
Yet knowing how way leads on to way
I doubted if I should ever come back.

I shall be telling this with a sigh
Somewhere ages and ages hence:
Two roads diverged in a wood, and I,
I took the one less traveled by,
And that has made all the difference

Notes

Day 12

Read Proverbs chapter 12.

Today, I want to spend more time on verse 10 (ESV): "Whoever is righteous has regard for the life of his beast, but the mercy of the wicked is cruel."

I grew up in a small town, and we lived on one of the busiest roads in town. We lived on a paved road, Benton Street, which was called by locals the Farm-to-Market Road. One of the draw backs of living on the road was losing pets. I sometimes joke about us living on such a busy road that we had a new dog every week. It wasn't that bad, but we did lose some and learned to be watchful of our pets.

When our children were growing up, my wife gave me a chocolate lab puppy for my birthday. Heath became an important part of our family, and we all became very attached to him. He was the smartest dog we ever had. When we get together with our children, as adults, we still tell Heath stories, and his memory is still a part of family gatherings.

I once heard a pastor talk about how your life changes when you become a "new creation," a Christian. He said even your pets will be able to notice your life is different. When I read this verse this morning, I thought perhaps I have found my basis for the truth of that sermon. As I go through this day, I pray my life will so reveal the presence of Christ that even a family pet would notice.

Which verse did you need to spend time on?

Notes

Day 13

Read Proverbs chapter 13.

Today, God is highlighting verses 7-8 (ESV): "One pretends to be rich, yet has nothing another pretends to be poor, ye has great wealth. "The ransom of a man's life is his wealth, but a poor man hears no threat."

Have you ever gotten to know a friend and been impressed with how unimportant wealth seems to him? I have been sensitive to this growing up poor in a small town. I delivered papers on the street where the wealthy people in the town lived. We called it "silk stocking row." I liked to trick-or-treat on the street because they gave out full-size candy bars.

I was impressed. I didn't have any friends at school on this street, and they would never invite someone like me into their home for a birthday party or to play. The people on the street were the hardest to collect payment from.

Last year, we visited the Walmart Museum in Arkansas. I have always been impressed with Sam Walton's life. We saw his old pickup truck that he loved to drive. It looked well cared for but an older model. He loved his truck and did not see a need to have a new one every few years. He could have bought a new truck every year, but that wasn't who he was.

A ransom is money paid to release a prisoner. Wealth can be something that imprisons you instead of blessing you.

One thing God has taught me this year is that God blesses me so I can bless others. I am blessed for a purpose and am not to be indulged, limited, and enslaved by wealth. I need to realize that no matter my level of wealth there are going to be many who have less and many who have more. It does not define me.

I need to realize that I leave this world the same way I came in: without owning any possessions. There isn't an earthly possession I can take with me. What I have use of is owned and given by God to be used for his purpose.

What verse did God highlight to you today?

Notes

Day 14

Read Proverbs chapter 14.

I am looking at verse 4 today (ESV): "Where there are no oxen, the manger is clean, but abundant crops come by the strength of the ox."

I worked in education for forty-four years. When I became a principal, I realized each job held contained some blinders to what was involved in other jobs. The reality of the job was different than the expectations.

As a new principal, I carefully planned my days with all I wanted to accomplish. What I found out was my days were full of interruptions that kept me from completing my plans. I felt like I was going around putting out little fires and if I ignored them or put them off they would grow into big fires.

One day, I read this verse, and it was an eye-opener. Work can be messy, but learning to clean up the mess is an important part of the job. Taking care of what is important may be hard but leads to an abundant crop.

I came to realize the interruptions were my real job and the other things were just things I needed to work in and get done. As I focused on these things as very important, the job went much better, and I had more time to get the other things done. The little fires did not become big fires, and they were less frequent as time went by.

God is so helpful through his Word, giving me new perspective to what is important and necessary.

What verse are you looking at today?

Notes

Day 15

Read Proverbs chapter 15.

Let's take a second look at verses 1-2 (ESV): "A soft answer turns away wrath, but a harsh word stirs up anger. The tongue of the wise commends knowledge, but the mouths of fools pour out folly."

I had this verse on my heart one day while sitting at my desk in my office. I had my door open listening as students passed in the hall. I was distracted from my work by overhearing an exchange between a junior high student and our computer technician. The tech was correcting a student, and the student was angrily talking back to him.

I interrupted the angry exchange, asked the student to step into my office without saying a word, sent the tech back to his room, and promised we would be by to visit soon. I asked the student to have a seat by my desk, and I sat down. I told him to sit and think about what happened and I had some work to finish and we would talk in a few minutes.

I pushed some papers around on my desk and silently prayed for wisdom. I watched the student's face slowly return to natural and his body relax into a normal posture. I asked him to listen and think while I said a few words.

"If I hadn't stopped the exchange, Mr. Smith would have brought you in through my open door with you both yelling at each other. If I had entered the conversation with a loud voice, think about what would have happened. It could have ended up in our calling your parents or, worse, a suspension, if you continued to talk back.

"None of that happened, and we can develop a new plan. Perhaps you would like us to walk down to Mr. Smith's room and apologize for what you were doing and the back talk. If you say it and mean it, I think he will be okay with you, and you can be back in your class in five minutes and finish the day without any more problems."

Then I listened to everything the student had to say, and we moved forward. I made it plain that Mr. Smith would make the decision if he was ready to return to class and his conversation needed to convince him that he was ready and his apology had to be authentic.

We went to Mr. Smith's room, and they had an honest conversation. He was respectful and back in his classroom for the rest of the day.

I think this scripture helped me think before I spoke. I would like to say that I operated like this example every day and didn't get caught up in the heat of the moment. I think you would know that isn't true, but my prayer is that God would remind me of the wisdom of the word often in my daily life.

What verse did you take a second look at today?

Notes

Day 16

Read Proverbs chapter 16.

Verse 20 is meaningful to me today (ESV): "Whoever gives thought to the word will discover good, and blessed is he who trusts in the Lord."

I love this verse! The purpose of this book is to get you hooked on a cool-of-the-day experience with the Lord, spending time with Him and learning the value of using His Word in a very practical way in your daily life.

My prayer is that you discover His Word is good and you will be blessed if you trust the Lord! I pray the applying of Proverbs is the beginning and takes you to a new view of the entire Bible and how relevant it is to your daily life. To learn to enjoy the presence of God so much that you long for it every day and through quiet moments throughout the day.

You come into His presence because you come to an understanding that he loves to spend time with you. He knows your needs before you ask, and your time with him is to get to know him better. You no longer need to come with just a list of needs and a scripture a day to keep the devil away. You come to fellowship!

"For I know the plans I have for you, declares the Lord, plans for welfare and not for evil, to give you a future and a hope" (Jeremiah 29:11, EVS).

What verse was meaningful to you today?

Notes

Day 17

Read Proverbs chapter 17.

I need verse 5 today (ESV): "Whoever mocks the poor insults the Maker; he who is glad at calamity will not go unpunished."

Have you ever stopped to think that the Bible teaches that our actions and attitudes toward each other reflect our attitudes to God? When we look down on, mock, or insult someone else, we are insulting their maker. God has given us the greatest example of love through His son, Jesus.

God's gift to man: "He has made everything beautiful in its time. Also, he has put eternity into man's heart, yet so he cannot find out what God has done from the beginning to the end. I perceived that there is nothing better for them than to be joyful and to do good as long as they live; also, that everyone should eat and drink and take pleasure in all his toil—that is God's gift to man" (Ecclesiastes 3:11-13, ESV).

God gives us plenty of reasons to have a good attitude and the best example of love for one another.

Which verse did you need today?

Notes

Day 18

Read Proverbs chapter 18.

I want to draw your attention to verses 2 and 10 (ESV): "A fool takes no pleasure in understanding, but only in expressing his opinion" and "The name of the Lord is a strong tower; the righteous man runs into it and is safe."

These two verses speak to me today. The Lord and the name of the Lord is a strong place where I can find safety. The Word of the Lord provides a standard of truth where I can find peace and safety. It can provide knowledge to be remembered, but that is only level 1, when you gain the knowledge during your cool-of-the-day experience with Jesus.

The Holy Spirit can take you to a deeper level where there is understanding with application to your daily life. If I operate on the remembering/understanding level, I am missing the point. It is not a life-changing experience.

The Sadducees were the Jewish sect that operated on the selective remembering/understanding level. The problem they created was they only believed in the Pentateuch (the first five books of the Bible). They did not believe the whole Bible. We remember them as liberal theologians who were selecting only the parts they wanted to believe and dismissing the parts they didn't want to affect their lives. We remember their name by thinking of them as sad-you-see. They missed the resurrection, the belief in heaven, the Messiah (Jesus), the deep personal relationship with a loving God, the hope of His second coming, and the peace that is beyond understanding.

It *is* sad! Don't you see this?

What verse were you drawn to today?

Notes

Day 19

Read Proverbs chapter 19.

I would like to take a second look at verse 17: "Whoever is generous to the poor lends to the Lord, and he will repay him for his deed."

If you have read to this place in the book, you know that I grew up very poor and I have a place in my heart for those who are poor. I also know that God has a place in his big wonderful heart for the poor and will repay you for being generous to the poor.

I am not looking at this for a dollar-per-dollar return but have found God has ways beyond my imagination to reward for giving. It inspires us to be creative in giving. You can give through your church benevolent fund. You can physically help by assembling and distributing gifts to the poor. You can give of your time to organize that help by sorting groceries, distributing groceries, ringing the bell for donations, purchasing an extra bag of groceries when you shop, cleaning out your pantry regularly for overstocked items, looking for items you have decided not to use, putting your closet hangers on backward at the beginning of each season and clothes at the end of the season hung backward were not worn and could be donated.

You get request by phone or mail for donations to the poor. Pray about them, and check to see what percentage of the organization funds goes for administrative cost. Pick organizations that have the highest percentages going to direct services for the poor. Put your money and goods where they will do the best for the poor.

I really must check myself. I could go on and on about this, but in summary, I just ask God for wisdom in this area. It is important to me, the money, goods, and time spent are a real help to the people God loves, and need it.

What verse did you take a second look at?

Notes

Day 20

Read Proverbs 20 today.

Let's look at verse 9 (ESV): "Who can say, 'I have made my heart pure; I am clean from my sin?'" This question speaks to me. It clearly is a hypothetical question. There is no answer to the question, or the answer is "No one." For the New Testament says in Romans 3:23, "For all have sinned and fall short of the Glory of God."

Our only hope of being clean from our sins is found in the glory of God, and that is His son, Jesus. If we trust in, rely upon, believe in, and have a relationship with Jesus, we can be free of our sin. He has paid the price for our sins, and we are forgiven. Our name is written in the Lamb's Book of Life. When God looks at us he does not see our sins. They are as far as the east is from the west. He sees the presence of Jesus in our life.

We sometimes have knowledge and belief in this, but we do not always walk in an understanding that we apply to our daily thinking and attitude. We still act like we must be good enough for God to love us or accept us. We sometimes think we need to get rid of certain sins before we can place our faith in Jesus and become a Christian.

Jesus of the New Testament, who is the same Jesus in our would today, offers a real "Just as I Am" offer today. Come just as you are today to him, and through your relationship with Him, you will work out the details together. Don't try to work them out on your own. You are wasting your time. You don't have the knowledge, power, or resources to do it by yourself.

In the presence of Jesus, you will find everything you need. I need to bring this hope to people whom I come into contact with today.

What verse did you look at today?

Notes

Day 21

Read chapter 21 in Proverbs today.

I would like to spend time on verse 13 (ESV) today: "Whoever closes his ear to the cry of the poor will himself call out and not be answered."

You can see how many verses apply to the poor, and I am drawn to think about them. I am getting to the point that I do not like to go to Walmart any more. As I drive out of the back of the lot and pass Wendy's to get to the main street, my eyes fall upon the intersection. They stand on the right where traffic must stop and wait for an opportunity to move. It may be a man who is asking for help for his daughter who has cancer, a couple with a child standing in the rain with a cardboard sign that says, "Homeless—Anything Will Help."

I could fill the rest of this page with descriptions. I do not often carry much cash because I get a percentage transferred to my savings account for all purchases. I have a no-interest credit card for eighteen months. When the free interest expires, I cancel the card and get another free-interest card because I do not want to pay interest to anyone. I am not a wealthy man, but I am comfortable.

As I drive by these people in my inexpensive Chevy Cruze, the difference between renting a small home, purchasing a small car, with all my bills paid on time and standing out in the weather holding a cardboard sign is huge. Having been a child of poverty, my heart breaks as I drive upon this scene.

I know what you may be thinking. I have seen the documentaries on TV showing the panhandlers and how they are too lazy to work, are mentally ill, need money for drugs, etc. I am setting in my warm car driving past, and my heart is breaking and I don't know what to do. The number of people in our community who do this has exploded in the last few years. I cannot drive into Springfield without seeing several corners with people holding signs.

I need to pray about what to do. I often feel I would rather be fooled than pass someone who is desperate, so I am asking God for help. Is this person in need or perhaps an angel who is testing the hearts of people in my community? "God, what should I do?"

If you have money to give, you can give. If you have no money, you can pray for them. You can pray that their real need that brought them to this point is met by God, who loves them the same as he loves you. Peter and John said, "Silver and gold have I none but such as I have give you, in the name of Jesus Christ rise up and walk" (KJ).

It is important that you care. You need to respond in some way. You can't just drive by with no response. If you see this throughout your community, you know they are not all false requests. God may be prompting you to give to organizations to help the homeless. They also need people to volunteer their time to help. Your contact will be more personal, and you will know their needs are real, and you can feel free to give.

I give to several organizations in my community and personally work in a food pantry storeroom sorting groceries. We also contribute groceries to a food pantry every month, and we donate items to a resell shop that supports families with needs. I pray about every encounter on the street and give when I can.

I can't tell you the answers I have found for me are the answers for you in your situation. I can say be sensitive to the needs of others, don't close your ears.

Notes

Day 22

Read Proverbs chapter 22.

Verses 6 and 15 (ESV) give me a similar message: "Train up a child in the way he should go; even when he is old he will not depart from it" and "Folly is bound up in the heart of a child, but the rod of discipline drives it far from him."

These verses may be new to you. If you grew up in church, you probably have heard them many times. Before I think about this, I want to think about three other scriptures today:

"Whoever spares the rod hates his son, but he who loves him is diligent to discipline him" (Proverbs 13:24, ESV).

"Fathers, do not provoke your children to anger, but bring them up in the discipline and instruction of the Lord" (Ephesians 6:4, ESV).

"But as you, continue in what you have learned and have firmly believed, knowing from whom you learned it and how from childhood you have been acquainted with the sacred writings, which are able to make you wise for salvation through faith in Christ Jesus. All Scripture is breathed out by God and profitable for teaching, for reproof, for correction, and for training in righteousness, that the man of God may be complete, equipped for every good work." 2 Timothy 3:15 (ESV)

I have been a parent for over forty-four years and a grandparent for fifteen. When God calls my thoughts to this, I must think about this in context of many things He has to say about raising children. If I love my children, I discipline them in the love that God teaches me to have for them. I have learned the difference between punishment and discipline. I have also learned the difference between discipline and discipline in love.

Think about Matthew 7:11: "If you then who are evil, know how to give good gifts to your children, how much more will our Father who is in heaven give good things to those who ask him!"

God is our example. I still love my children the same as when God gave them to us as babies. When their life is good, my life is good. When they hurt, I hurt, and I am on my face in the floor before God.

Notes

Day 23

Read Proverbs chapter 23.

I need to spend more time with verses 17 and 18 (ESV): "Let not your heart envy sinners, but continue in the fear of the Lord all the day. Surely there is a future, and your hope will not be cut off."

These verses remind me of times in my life I took my eyes off the Lord and began to look at others. I began to make comparisons and began to think about the influence of some I knew. They seemed to have so much and have no regard or time for the Lord. You start to look at the possessions and positions of others, and envy can take you to a dark place.

The fear of the Lord is the answer. When I saw that word translated as fear, I looked it up to see the original word. If it is *yirah*, as it is in this verse, it means more than our concept of fear. It means reverence, awe, and to recognize God as all-powerful in a way that is reflected in our daily life.

I need to get my eyes on Jesus and realize my hope and future are in him. As I talk to the Lord about a verse, I see He wants me to think and He also reminds me of other verses I need to think about. I think about Psalm 25:14 (ESV): "The friendship of the Lord is for those who fear him, and he makes known to them his covenant."

"Fret not yourself because of evildoers; be not envious of wrongdoers; For they will soon fade like the grass and wither like the green herb" (Psalm 37:1-2).

The more of his Word I learn, the more He can use it to enrich our relationship and my life.

Notes

Day 24

Read Proverbs chapter 24.

Let's look at verses 5 and 6 (ESV): "A wise man is full of strength, and a man of knowledge enhances his might, for by wise guidance you can wage your war, and in abundance of counselors there is victory."

The real strength of a man of God comes from the wisdom of God. It is to be valued. This verse also speaks to me of the need to understand we are involved in a war and the importance of godly counsel.

If you are looking at life through your natural eyes, you may be unaware of the guidance you need to wage your war. Yes, it says, "Your war." We each have a war to fight with many battles. It is not a war of flesh and blood but a war in the spiritual realm. With our spiritual eyes, we can become very aware of the darts of the enemy. We gain this view through the Word of God, the presence of the great counselor (the Holy Spirit), and the counsel of Christian friends.

This makes me aware of the need for Christian friends and their counsel in my life. I am to seek godly counsel and give godly counsel when called upon. I need to realize my spiritual war is a personal war with the enemy who is attempting to rob, kill, and destroy.

I also realize I have many great resources in this battle. If I seek the Lord, He will be found and provide the help I need to overcome. I need to walk into this day with my spiritual eyes open.

Notes

Day 25

Read Proverbs chapter 25.

I need to look at verses 16 and 27-28 (ESV):

If you found honey, eat only enough for you, lest you have your fill of it and vomit it." And "It is not good to eat much honey, nor is it glorious to seek one's own glory. A man without self-control is like a city broken into and left without walls.

If you look at our picture on the back cover of this book, you see us as we are today, give or take 10 pounds. After losing 125 pounds, I am so aware of the number of people in our country who struggle with their weight and the effects it has upon their health.

I had reached a point where I weighed almost 300 pounds and was afraid to weigh myself. I was taking three pills a day for diabetes, and my sugar level was out of control. My doctor was ready to put me on insulin for my diabetes. My blood pressure was out of control, and I was taking two kinds of blood pressure medication.

My wife is a registered nurse, and her weight was also out of control. We tried every weight loss plan we could find, losing as much as 40 pounds at a time and then quickly regaining it.

When I walk through the airport and see the vast number of overweight people, I do not look at them with scorn or look down on them. I know how they feel. I know how it feels to be trapped in my own body. We had to take extreme measures and get help from outside ourselves.

We studied gastric bypass surgery for a year and found a wonderful surgeon who was an expert in the area. He had performed hundreds of surgeries and has very strict procedures to be followed to qualify for the surgery or he would not operate.

I would like to tell you we said a prayer and our gluttony just went away. That can certainly happen for people, but we were very far gone, and although our God is able, we were not, and had to reach out to others for help.

In 2009 we both had Roux-en-Y gastric bypass surgery because at the time research said it was best for diabetics. Jan lost over 100 pounds, and I lost over 125 pounds. Since my surgery, I have not taken any medicine for my diabetes, and my sugar levels have been stable for all these years.

At my last physical, my doctor said, "You are not a diabetic because your three-month A1C is perfect." I take one pill a day for blood pressure to keep my pressure lower than normal because of an aortic valve birth defect, and the pressure has remained normal since my surgery.

I don't know why I shared all this grit except many people in this life find themselves in desperate situations. My desperate situation that was killing me had to do with food, but it could be caused by many things.

If you are in a desperate situation, pray for God to show you where help will be found, and ask him to give you the courage to step out and let others help. God can provide sources of help beyond your own resources and give you the courage to let them help you.

I do not look down on people in desperate situations. I pray fervently for them and know I serve a God who loves them and cares about every detail in their lives. His answers for you will be unique and specifically designed for your situation. Rest in the confidence He is the source where answers are found.

Notes

Day 26

Read Proverbs chapter 26.

I want to take a second look at verse 2 (ESV) today: "Like a sparrow, in its flitting, like a swallow in its flying, a curse that is causeless does not alight."

"Like the sparrow in her wandering, like the swallow in her flying so the causeless curse does not alight" Proverbs 26:2 (Amplified).

I'm sure you have figured out that I love to read the ESV version of the Bible. Sometimes a verse does not seem clear to me, so I read from my Comparative Study Bible. It has side-by-side translations from King James, Amplified, New American Standard, and New International. I can usually get a better idea about a passage I am not sure I understand.

My ESV has cross-references, which lead me to related passages, and I sometimes check them. This usually happens on days when I have a little extra time and God leads me into a deeper study.

"But the Lord your God would not listen to Balaam; instead the Lord your God turned the curse into a blessing for you, because the Lord your God loved you" (Deuteronomy 23:5).

"It may be that the Lord will look on the wrong done to me, and that the Lord will repay me with good for his cursing today" (2 Samuel 16:12).

These verses say to me today that I do not have to fear when men curse me and try to work evil against me. My God loves me, and he protects me. He turns what is meant for evil to work for my good. He sends angels to guard and protect me. He reminds me that what I see with my eyes is this world, and it is not permanent. What I can't see with these eyes is the spiritual world, and it *is* permanent.

Notes

Day 27

Read Proverbs chapter 27.

I am going to study verse 17 (ESV): "Iron sharpens iron, and one man sharpens another."

The Word is saying to me that one man should improve the countenance of his friend. We should be a strength and be building each other up. Jesus is a friend who sticks closer than a brother. The Bible says he was God and man. He was tempted in all ways like any man yet was sinless. No one can understand and help like Jesus. One man can be a help and strength for his friend.

Through the years, we have worked and lived in several locations. We have always been a part of the local church. In the churches, the women's organizations have always been much stronger than the men's. This has always bothered me, and I have always thought it should be the opposite.

One of the main purposes of this book is to get men hooked on daily spending time in the Word and developing powerful cool-of-the-day experiences with Jesus. The stronger the relationship becomes, the stronger the man will become. The better men become at helping each other, the stronger the local church will be.

It is important to have a circle of men you fellowship with who encourage each other. We all need prayer partners and friends to meet for coffee and encouragement.

Notes

Day 28

Read Proverbs chapter 28.

I want to look closer at verse 9 (ESV): "If one turns away his ear from hearing the law, even his prayer is an abomination."

The Amplified Bible implies "the law" in this verse means God's law and man's law. I guess this verse spoke to me today because I see many news shows about people gathering in groups to protest, but instead of protesting peacefully, they begin breaking out windows, hurting others, and stealing from stores. They destroy the message they are trying to send by protesting.

I know there are other verses from the Bible that talk about God not hearing our prayer: "If I had cherished iniquity in my heart, the Lord would not have listened" (Psalm 66:18, ESV) and "When he is tried, let him come forth guilty, let his prayer be counted as sin" (Psalm 109:7, ESV).

I know from scripture that God does want me to listen to his law and the law of man. I can put myself in danger of my prayers not being heard. During my cool-of-the-day experience with my Lord, I need to talk with Him about this from time to time to make sure the lines of communication are open.

Notes

Day 29

Read Proverbs chapter 29.

Verse 1 (ESV) is important to me today: "He who is often reproved, yet stiffens his neck, will suddenly be broke beyond healing."

This proverb speaks to me about the powerful importance of my response when I am corrected by man or God. Especially by God, because he is always truthful, and his reproof is needed and should be welcomed. It is a path to healing and peace of mind.

A stiffened neck as a response to reproof can lead to a pattern-developed response. The more you respond this way, the stronger the response reflex becomes. Each response develops a scar, and over time, you do not hear the rebuke and are beyond healing.

God's Word is true, and this is a very serious warning that needs to be taken to heart. It reminds me of the situation Pharaoh was in with Moses. As each rebuke from God brought plagues to his land, he became angrier, and hardened his heart. It eventually led to his destruction and the destruction of his entire army.

I am also reminded of a very different story when Naaman came to talk to David. He told David the story of a man who was horrible and caused harm and death to a man who did not deserve it. David's response was that man should be punished. When Naaman said, "You are that man," everything was on the line.

David knew his sins with Bathsheba and sending her husband to be killed to cover up his adultery and child on the way was exposed. He had a choice of how to respond. David was not a perfect servant; in fact, he was very flawed. He did love God and was sorry for his sins.

His response was, "You are right I am that man, and deserve to be punished by God." He admitted his sins and did suffer punishment for them. He went on to become a great leader for God, and the Bible says he was a man after God's own heart.

Today I want to think about that. I want to admit I have sin in my life. When God confronts me with sin, I want to be honest about it and learn from it to be more of what God wants me to be.

I know the danger of stiffening my neck. It's hard for a man to admit this. It's hard for *me* to admit this.

Notes

Day 30

Read Proverbs chapter 30.

Today, I will focus on verses 7-9 (ESV): "Two things I ask of you; deny them not to me before I die: remove far from me falsehood and lying; give me neither poverty nor riches; feed me with the food that is needful for me, lest I be full and deny you and say, 'Who is the Lord?' or lest I be poor and steal and profane the name of my God."

I have heard this proverb quoted in many ways. Some say, "Lord, make me rich enough to meet my needs and never so poor that I steal food and dishonor you." I'm sure you have heard some version. Although Solomon predates Confucius and most philosophers who are often quoted, he is often not credited for saying many profound things.

This day, as I think about this proverb, I realize that living in America I really need this. Our country is so affluent compared to most of the world. Even the poverty level in America is far above the standard of living for most of the people in the world. The things we worry over are beyond the imagination of many. I am humbled when God brings this to my attention. I need to spend the day counting my blessings.

One day, during my cool-of-the-day experiences, I realized I read the Word of God through the filter of my life experiences and my culture. I asked God to speak to me plainly about what my Christian life should look like if I did not filter his Word through my culture. I just stopped walking and listened for a long time.

I didn't hear an audible voice, but in that still quiet, knowing He speaks to our spirit, I came to the realization that this would be a huge shock to me and my system. I could not handle it all at once. He would have to take me step by step if I was willing to travel this road.

Part of me was very hurt that I was very far from where I should be and so tarnished by my experiences and culture. Part of me was so grateful that I serve a loving and patient God.

Notes

Day 31

Read chapter 31.

I am looking at verses 4-5 (ESV): "It is not for kings, O Lemuel, it is not for kings to drink wine, or for rulers to take strong drink. Lest they drink and forget what has been decreed and pervert the rights of all the afflicted."

I think this is an interesting warning against the use of wine and strong drink. It can affect the ability to make good decisions that can be harmful to large numbers of people. In the context of their culture, it seems to be a warning of just drinking wine by itself away from meals for the effect of wine and strong drink. It is not okay for a king to do this. It was the evidence that a king was a bad king.

How does this apply to me? How does this apply to you? My decisions don't affect large numbers of people throughout a country. My decisions directly affect the ones I love, and that makes this warning just as important.

I think this is good advice. God knows what is best for me.

Notes

CHAPTER 3

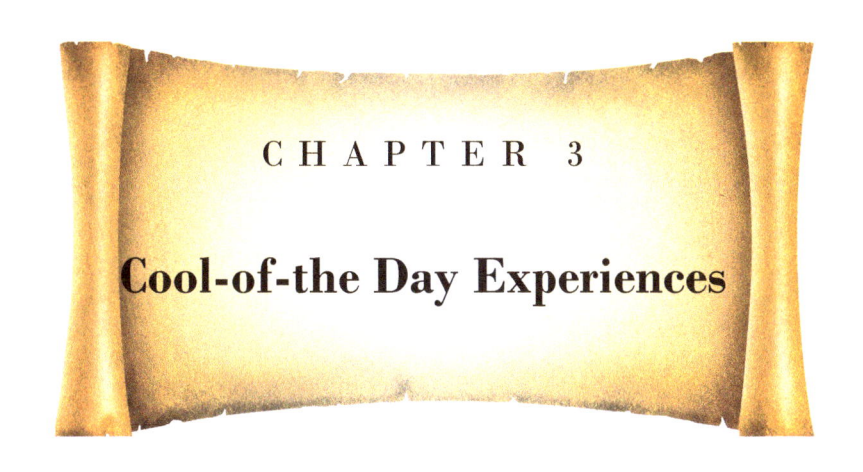

Cool-of-the Day Experiences

Cool-of-the-Day Experience

"And they heard the sound of the Lord God walking in the garden in the cool of the day ..." (Genesis 3:8, ESV).

We know from scripture that God came to visit with Adam and Eve in the garden before the fall, which caused a great separation between man and God. When God's son, Jesus, came to sacrifice Himself for our sin, he also created the opportunity for the cool-of-the-day experience.

When we have Jesus in our life and the Father looks at us, He sees Jesus. Our sins are forgiven and covered by his presence in our lives. He has restored our relationship with God, and he desires us to love him enough to spend time with Him. It is important that during my time with God I listen for Him to speak to me. "Everyone who hears these words of mine and puts them in practice is like a wise man" (Matthew 7:24). How can I do this unless I listen and spend time in his Word?

After spending daily time with God, I have learned to enjoy His presence and look forward to our time together. There are many reasons this time has become important to me: (1) God established it with Adam and Eve, (2) I have learned that He desires to have fellowship and friendship with me, (3) He sent Jesus to provide our salvation and restore the intimate communication with me, (4) Psalm 25:14: "The friendship of the Lord is for those who fear him and He makes known to them His covenant," (5) the friendship of the Lord is available to everyone who is a Christian, and (6) the friendship of the Lord is cultivated during the time spent with him.

I am constantly learning reasons for this time to be important and beneficial to me.

There is an old hymn, "In the Garden" by C. Austin Miles, that means so much to me. I remember it from my childhood, and it speaks to me about my special time spent with the Lord:

I come to the garden alone
While the dew is still on the roses
And the voice I hear
Falling from my ear,
The Son of God discloses.

-

Verse
And He walks with me
And he talks with me.
And he tells me I am his own;
And the joy we share as we tarry there,
None other has ever known.

-

He speaks, and the sound of His voice
Is so sweet the birds hush their singing,
And the melody That He gave to me,
With in my heart is ringing.

-

I'd stay in the garden with Him
Though the night a round me be falling,
But He bids me go;
Tho' the voice of woe
His voice to me is calling

Describe your daily time with God after working through this book. What has it come to mean to you? (If you do not know the song, you can go to YouTube and listen to it.)

Being Saved

When I was a child, I had a salvation experience in Vacation Bible School. I was probably six or seven years old. I did not understand much. I remember the drawing of the Holy Spirit and understood that I did wrong things and had sin in my life. I remember asking for forgiveness and making promises to follow Jesus.

I knew I was saved. I was not baptized at that time because my mother felt I was too young to understand. I began to read my Bible and pray each night before I went to sleep. I thought my salvation was an experience or event that had happened to me.

During my freshman year in college, I felt the drawing of the Holy Spirit to make an adult commitment to Christ and be baptized. I made this commitment of faith and action that opened a door to a daily experience with God that was more than reading my Bible and prayer before I went to sleep.

I had a red-letter edition of the Bible and understood the words of Jesus were written in red. I wanted to know every word he spoke, and the Bible became alive to me. These words Jesus actually spoke, and I wanted to know and understand every word.

I began to really understand the "believe" of John 3:16 (KJ): "For God so loved the world that He gave His only begotten son, that whosoever believed in him shall not perish, but have everlasting life."

Through spending time in his Word, I began to understand *believe* meant trust in, adhere to, and rely upon Him. I also came to understand that "be saved" meant "being saved." Salvation was not an experience but an experience-filled life. I was "being saved," and that involved a relationship with Jesus.

I learned that this is a process that began with a salvation experience, but I would have opportunity, the resources, and the relationship to know this was not a religion but a relationship with Christ. I also learned that a relationship takes an investment of time. For a relationship to grow, you need to spend time together. It takes time for love and understanding to develop.

My cool-of-the-day experience has opened my eyes to so many wonderful things about God. His love, grace, and mercy are truly amazing.

Write about being saved and what this has come to mean to you:

Abba Father

At the beginning of this book, I shared some of my childhood experiences with my father leaving my family when I was very young. I understand the impact that has on a child's self-concept. I know how it feels to grow up with the haunting questions it creates: "Why did he leave? Why didn't he love me? What was wrong with me that he didn't love me?"

The pattern is common for children deserted by a parent. It points to a hole in your self-confidence that can deeply affect the way you view yourself and your ability to trust others.

One night, in my time with God, he brought me to Romans 8:14-17 (ESV): "For all who are led by the Spirit of God are sons of God. For you did not receive the spirit of slavery to fall back into fear, but you have received the spirit of adoption as sons, by whom we cry. Abba! Father! The Spirit himself bears witness with our spirit that we are children of God, and if children, the heirs—heirs of God and fellow heirs with Christ, provided we suffer with him in order that we may also be glorified with him."

Mark 14:36 (ESV) says, "And he [Jesus] said, Abba, Father, all things are possible for you, Remove this cup from me. Yet not what I will, but what you will."

"And because you are sons God has sent the spirit of his Son into our hearts, crying Abba! Father! So, you are no longer a slave, but a son, and if a son, then an heir through God" (Galatians 4:6, ESV).

The concept of Abba Father-Daddy became very real to me. I was not a slave to my thoughts and feelings, and a big hole in my heart was being filled with the understanding of who I was in Christ Jesus. I was crawling up in Daddy's lap. Abba was an intimate term for God as Father.

The Holy Spirit came to minister to me about the meaning of these scriptures. I was never alone when I felt alone. I was always loved even when I was not feeling it. God created me for a purpose and loved me beyond my ability to understand love. There wasn't something wrong with me because my father did not love me.

There was something wrong with my earthly father because he didn't have the ability to love me. There was a hole in his heart. I did not have to be like him. I could be like my Heavenly Father and love like my Abba Father. I could forgive my earthly father and pray for him that someday he might be made whole through a relationship with Jesus that is available to all men.

It was such a healing experience that as a grown man I cried like a baby but got up from that time of prayer a whole person.

I was always delighted when my children came by my work to visit me. If my door was open, they knew I was not in conference with anyone. They would buzz by my secretary and say, "Is my dad in his office?" They knew if I was there that they had access to their father. It never occurred to them to ask permission; it was just understood. They always had access to their father, and I understood that I always have access to the Father through his, Son Jesus Christ. It gives me great joy for the privilege of spending time with Him. His love for me is extravagant!

Notes

Forgiveness

Through my daily walks with Christ, I see He has taught me many things about the power of forgiveness. Understanding forgiveness is a key to my developing a relationship with Christ. He is all about forgiveness. My salvation is based upon my belief that Jesus is the Son of God and has given his life as a sacrifice for my sins. I am forgiven and He is the example and commands me to forgive. "And forgive us our debts, as we forgive our debtors" (Matthew 6:12, ESV).

I have come to realize when I pray the prayer Jesus modeled for us that I am asking Him to forgive me the same as I am forgiving others. If I am not a forgiving person, I am asking him not to forgive me. "For if you forgive others their trespasses, your heavenly Father will also forgive you, but if you do not forgive others their trespasses, neither will your Father forgive your trespasses" (Matthew 6:14-15, ESV).

As I began to understand forgiveness, I realized it was a door to freedom. Holding on to anger and a grudge are not harmful to the person you are not forgiving; it destroys you. It eats away at you and robs you of your health and peace of mind. Learning to forgive and leave things in God's hand is liberating.

God brought this home to me in a very personal way. I became very concerned about my father's salvation and one of the most important things the Lord taught me was I needed to forgive him if I ever hoped he would believe he could find forgiveness through his relationship with Jesus. The most powerful way to lead him to believe he could be forgiven is by demonstrating forgiveness to him. Why should he ever believe what I am saying if I can't demonstrate that forgiveness is real?

I said, *"Oh, God, you don't know what you are asking,"* and his *answer through His Word was that he understood by being willing to give his only son so I could be forgiven. I spoke to my dad many times about giving his heart to Jesus, and when he told me I could not talk to him about this anymore, I would write him letters telling him how much God loved him and how much I loved him and wanted him to be saved.*

To my knowledge, he never made that decision. He was the son of a minister, and he still would not accept. When he died, I stood at his coffin and prayed. "God, I did not really know this man or understand him. He is my earthly father, and I don't know how I am supposed to feel at his passing. It is like the passing of a stranger. I do have a peace of mind that comes only from you. I have done as you asked me to do.

"I have forgiven him and tried my best to lead him to you. I leave him in your hands not knowing, and I thank you for the peace that comes from you while I am going through this experience. I do not understand. You are my kind and loving Heavenly Father. Someday I will be with you, and then I will understand. Until then, I trust."

Forgiveness is the door to understanding God and the path to peace beyond our own understanding.

How does forgiveness in your life help you understand being saved? Is there anything you need to do in this area of your life?

Vain Imaginations

"We destroy arguments and every lofty opinion raised against the knowledge of God, and take every thought captive to obey Christ" (2 Corinthians 10:5, ESV).

During my time with God, He has taught me a great deal about taking thoughts captive. Spending time with God creates a solid framework for evaluating ideas that come my way. We get information from many different directions: the media, other people, our own thoughts, and God's Word. Taking thoughts captive applies to all areas but especially when you are talking to yourself. My thoughts can go off in many wild directions. God is teaching me to send then through the filter created by God's Word and time spent with Him.

I am constantly learning about taking thoughts captive and making choices against vain imaginations. They are such a waste of time and source of distraction from the truth. God encourages me to make choices lined up with his ways.

I have wasted much time thinking about what others might think or what they might mean by things they said. I am learning to trust God and depend on the Holy Spirit to give me words to say instead of spending time planning and planning and imagining words, thoughts, and motives that usually are not helpful. I make deliberate choices to think positively about people until I am forced to think otherwise. I am becoming more aware of conversations to be avoided and the strength to divert from them.

The ability to take thoughts captive is a powerful tool when forgiving others. I am learning to not participate in negative conversations. I need to be talking to God and get wisdom and peace from him. This is one of the best lessons God teaches me. It is a practical path to peace of mind.

How can biblical principles of dealing with vain imaginations bring you into a closer fellowship with God?

No Condemnation

"For God did not send his Son into the world to condemn the world, but in order that the world might be saved through him" (John 3:17, ESV).

"There is therefore now no condemnation for those who are in Christ Jesus. For the law of the Spirit of life has set you free in Christ Jesus from the law of sin and death. For God has done what the law, weakened by the flesh, could not do. By sending his own Son in the likeness of sinful flesh and for sin, in order that the righteous requirement of the law might be fulfilled in us, who walk not according to the flesh but according to the Spirit" (Romans 8:1-4, ESV).

During my time with God and his Word, I have learned that believing in, trusting, and adhering to Jesus also means I accept being set free from the law by the Spirit of life in Christ Jesus. For God has done what the law, weakened by the flesh, could not do. He sent his own Son in the likeness of sinful flesh and for sin, in order that the righteous requirement of the law might be fulfilled in us, who walk not according to the flesh but according to the Spirit.

I have learned that believing in Jesus also means accepting the forgiveness of sin through Jesus's sacrifice. To know that forgiveness means your sins are as far as the east is from the west (from Psalm 103:12).

You must work out your salvation with fear (respect) and trembling (deep respect) (from Philippians 2:12). My pastor says you are saved from sin past, present, and future. It is not a license to sin and recognize that saved people do not want to sin, but as flawed people, we do sin but try our best not to sin. We can be secure in our walk. We can know that we know we know we are saved through our relationship with Jesus.

Accepting Jesus is accepting the "No condemnation" part. He offers the peace of mind that this world apart from him can never give. The more time you spend with Him, the more your confidence grows. You spend time with people you want to know. It is impossible to know someone well you don't spend time with.

What does the concept of "No condemnation" mean to you in your daily walk with the Lord?

Beside Still Waters

"He makes me lie down in green pastures, *He leads me beside still waters. He restores my soul.* He leads me in the paths of righteousness for his name sake" (Psalm 23:1-3, ESV; emphasis added).

The more cool-of-the-day experiences you have, the more you understand the need to spend time with God. You begin to make connections between spending time with Him in the Word with the events in you daily life. This scripture is one of the most familiar passages in the Bible.

Sheep will not drink from running water. They are afraid of running water and drowning. The shepherd is aware of the need of his sheep. The Lord is aware of our needs for still water and restoration.

I pray for quiet moments during my day to mentally lie in green pastures beside still waters, which are quiet pools of time during my day. Time to think about the Lord and for him to bring to my remembrance what I need during the day. Time to just say how thankful I am for his presence in my life. These experiences are restoring my soul, acknowledging His presence in my day.

I need to go through my day with an expectation that He is interested in the details of my life. I am not alone. How can you find green pastures and times of still waters throughout your day? How can you "put on Jesus"?

"But put on the Lord Jesus Christ, and make no provision for the flesh, to gratify its desires" (Romans 13:14, ESV).

He is willing to give help as needed and stick closer than a brother (from Proverbs 16:24). His love for me is extravagant.

What does it mean to "put on" the Lord Jesus Christ?

Renewing Your Mind

"I appeal to you therefore, brothers, by the mercies of God, to present your bodies as a living sacrifice, holy and acceptable to God, which is your spiritual worship. Do not be conformed to this world, but *be transformed by the renewal of your mind*, that by testing you may discern what is the will of God, what is good and acceptable and perfect" (Romans 12:1-2, ESV).

I find a great deal of comfort in this scripture. As I spend more time with Christ, I see He can be renewing my mind and increasing my ability to discern his will is exciting. His ways are higher than my ways. He always tells the truth. As I seek the mind of Christ, I can learn what is good and acceptable and perfect in His eyes (from 1 Corinthians 2:16).

When the enemy offers the ways of this world, I need to recognize it. If I let it into my life, it causes scars that make it hard to understand and follow the ways of God. If I spend time with God and practice his ways in my daily life, these scars can be healed. My mind can be renewed (reprogramed) to walk the path that He has planned for me. God loves me and has a wonderful plan for my life.

God asked Solomon what he wanted if he could have anything, and this is his response: "Give your servant therefore an understanding mind to govern your people, that I may discern between good and evil, for who is able to govern this your great people. It pleased the Lord that Solomon had asked this" (1 Kings 3:9-10, ESV).

"For I know the plans I have for you, declares the Lord, plans for welfare and not for evil, to give you a future and a hope" (Jeremiah 29:11, ESV).

I recognize God has my welfare in mind, and I place my hope in him today.

If you could ask God for anything, what would you ask for?

Fear Not

When the angel announced the birth of Christ, he said in Luke 2:10 (ESV), "Fear not, for behold I bring you good news of great joy that will be for all the people."

"Fear not" is one of the most repeated statements in the Bible. Jesus said in John 14:1-4, "Let not your heart be troubled. Believe in God; believe also in me. In my Father's house are many rooms. If it were not so, would I have told you that, I go to prepare a place for you. And if I go and prepare a place for you, I will come again and will take you to myself, that where I am you may be also. And you know the way to where I am going."

When you read all the "Fear nots" expressed in the Bible and you read the words of Jesus telling us not to be troubled, you develop a real warm and welcoming relationship with Him. When you read all the verses about how much God loves us and desires to fellowship with us, you come to know him.

When you read all the names for God in the Bible, you begin to understand that each name stands for a wonderful character trait of God. Some examples are provider, healer, counselor, savior, creator, most high, etc. The early Hebrew scribes so reverenced God they would not even say his name out loud. They knew how awesome, powerful, and loving He is.

Spending time with a loving God is a great privilege. As I go through this day, I want to be thankful I do not have to live in fear.

"For the righteous will never be moved; he will be remembered forever. He is not afraid of bad news; his heart is firm, trusting in the Lord" (Psalm 112:6-7).

How can you live a life without fear?

All Things Work Together for Good

"And we know that for those who love God all things work together for good, for those who are called according to his purpose" (Romans 8:28).

This verse does not say everything that happens to us was good, but if we love God, they can work for our good. There were many unpleasant things that happened during my life. As I learned to accept the love of God, He brought healing for these experiences.

I believe I could use these experiences to be a better counselor to children. I worked several years as a school counselor and a guidance director. I felt God used the things from my youth to be of help to others. If you have experienced something someone is going through, you can look them in the face and they know you understand like no one else can. If you let Him, God can use this for His purpose, and this can be part of his healing for you. That is what I experienced during those years.

Sometimes, I was sent on a path of learning things that God knew I would need in the future. I went through my own midlife crises during my late forties. I was restless and didn't know if I still wanted to be a teacher. I thought I would be happy being a certified public accountant.

I had a bachelor's degree and master's degree in education but went back to the local junior college and took all the accounting classes they offered. I also took some advanced classes to prepare for the CPA exam. When I began to look at entry-level CPA jobs, I realized I would be making a lot less than I currently made. My daughter was getting ready to go to college. I thought that was a fine time to figure how impracticable all this journey through accounting was about.

I bought a little red manual transmission car that I loved to drive. My wife said I could have the little red car but could not have a little young replacement to go in it. I guess I thought the accounting and car were a safe diversion of midlife, and I returned to concentrating on education as my profession.

God restored the love of my job to me and it was years later that I realized what God was doing. He was keeping me busy and from making some stupid mistakes that some men make at that age. He was also providing an opportunity to secure part-time accounting jobs to supplement my income while my daughter was in college.

It wasn't until I became a superintendent and had to create a school budget each year involving millions of dollars that I realized what a wonderful thing he had led me though. School finance is complicated, and your budget has several funds that run separately. The laws are specific about how each fund can be used and not comingled.

I realized the value of the accounting classes, and I said, "Thank you, God, for channeling my restlessness down a path that would be so helpful for the future you had planned for me. All these things are working together for my God. Your love is so awesome." I look at each day now and realize how he has prepared me to be at this stage of my life.

How are all things working together for your good when you love God and are called according to His purpose?

Knowing the Will of God

"The friendship of the Lord is for those who fear him, and he makes known to them his covenant" (Psalms 25:14, ESV).

A covenant is an agreement, a contract, and a plan. If God is my friend, I am spending time with him and respecting what He has to say. I am in His Word, and relating it to my daily life, and He is making known to me the plans He has for me. He has made plans for me before I was born. Being my creator, he has intimate details that are known by no one else. He even knows the number of hairs on my head that seem to be easier to count as each year goes by.

I find comfort in Psalm 37:23 (ESV): "The steps of a man are established by the Lord, when he delights in his ways; though he fall, he shall not be cast headlong, for the Lord upholds his hand."

Psalm 139:1-6 (ESV) tells me how well God knows me: "O'Lord you have searched me and known me! You know when I set down and when I rise up; you discern my thoughts from afar. You search out my path and my lying down and are acquainted with all my ways. Even before a word is on my tongue, behold, O'Lord, you know it altogether. You hem me in, behind and before, and lay your hand upon me. Such knowledge is too wonderful for me. It is high; I cannot attain it."

There was a time in my life I was not ready for this scripture, and it would have been frightening to know how much the Lord knew and was intimately aware of me and my thoughts. Now I find it so comforting.

It isn't that I've attained any perfection. I have attained an understanding of how deeply he loves me and how great His capacity for love is to care so much for a person like me. I trust him with this knowledge for my good. He is my creator.

I feel that God is so involved in my life that He comes to visit my pastor on Saturday afternoons and says, "Glen is going to be in church tomorrow, and here is what He needs you to say." I just go expecting God to speak to me. God knows my name, and He has written it in the Lamb's Book of Life. As Beth Moore says, "If nothing else good ever happens to me in this life, I am still blessed because my name is written down in the Lamb's Book of Life." That book will be open someday and read, and I think it will be soon.

"The two most important days of your life are when you are born and when you know why you were born" (David Lindell).

What are some things God is speaking to you about today?